PRENTICE-HALL

Foundations of World Regional Geography Series

PHILLIP BACON *and* LORRIN KENNAMER, *Editors*

GEOGRAPHY OF ANGLO-AMERICA, *Loyal Durand, Jr.*

GEOGRAPHY OF NORTH AFRICA AND SOUTHWEST ASIA,
   Paul W. English

GEOGRAPHY OF THE U.S.S.R., *W. A. Douglas Jackson*

GEOGRAPHY OF EUROPE, *Vincent H. Malmstrom*

SOUTHEAST ASIA, *Joseph E. Spencer*

GEOGRAPHY OF LATIN AMERICA, *Kempton E. Webb*

Foundations of World Regional Geography Series

Australia's Corner of the World

A GEOGRAPHICAL SUMMATION

THOMAS L. McKNIGHT

University of California at Los Angeles

PRENTICE-HALL, INC., Englewood Cliffs, N.J.

13-053801-9
13-053819-1

Library of Congress Catalog Card No: 73-104897

Current printing (last digit):
10 9 8 7 6 5 4 3 2 1

PRENTICE-HALL INTERNATIONAL, INC., London
PRENTICE-HALL OF AUSTRALIA, PTY., LTD., Sydney
PRENTICE-HALL OF CANADA, LTD., Toronto
PRENTICE-HALL OF INDIA PRIVATE LIMITED, New Delhi
PRENTICE-HALL OF JAPAN, INC., Tokyo

Preface

In an age of televised moon strolls, the words *terrae incognitae*, when applied to a major portion of planet Earth, seem at first thought strikingly anachronistic. And, of course, for most of us the idea of *terrae incognitae* is, indeed, an early nineteenth century notion that holds little promise of explaining men's views of a late twentieth century world. Nonetheless, these words may be particularly apt when applied to Australia's corner of the world, for surely there are few other areas of continental size on our inhabited earth that are more poorly understood.

What sorts of images are conjured up when Australia looms into view as one turns his globe to the watery hemisphere of the Pacific? Characteristically, even in Australia itself, the chief image is one of "the bush." Here are landscapes of dusty browns and reds, a gigantic pastureland occupied by mobs of sheep, all supervised by the legendary Australian—a tall, lean, sunburned, out-going, self-reliant, digger-hatted man of the Outback. Australia's literature, art, and music have all served to enforce this stereotype. Unfortunately, so has the physical, biotic, and cultural habitats described and interpreted in scores of school and introductory level college textbooks. Perhaps it is the neat arrangement of physical and biotic patterns, coupled with the export dominance of products of the land, that has led to many of the all too simple generalizations about the men and land of Australia.

Legends to the contrary, the Australian is a man of the city, and curiously, he always has been. From its very beginings, Australia has been a nation of urban dwellers. It may well be that the city is Australia's true frontier, for the population of no other major nation of the world is quite so citified.

Trying to balance the bush and the city in making an analysis of the *real* regional geography of Australia's corner of the world requires special talent. It seems to call for a geographer who is comfortable with the city and industrial development as well as with the open land beyond. Few can match Tom McKnight in this regard. His studies of manufacturing and of feral livestock have invested Professor McKnight with academic distinction. Such studies, made first in the United States, were carried to Australia where he has traveled, researched, written, and taught. Happily, Professor McKnight has, in addition to recognized scholarly competence, a genuine affinity for the place and the people. He has succeeded ably in this first volume of the Prentice-Hall World Regional Geography Series in pulling together the best of scholarship and personal perception—as the Australian would put it, in giving this part of the world "a fair go."

PHILLIP BACON
University of Washington

LORRIN KENNAMER
Texas Tech University

Contents

Figures

Tables

to Adelaide, a personal lodestone . . .

CHAPTER 1

the pacific setting of australia

The largest body of water known to man extends from the Arctic beaches of the Bering Sea in the north to the icy margins of Antarctica's Ross Sea in the south. On the east and west it washes the shores of four great land masses. Only Africa and Europe among the seven recognized continents do not lie on its fringes.

This ocean, known since the early 1500's as the Pacific, is the vastest and most conspicuous feature of our planet. With an extent of nearly 65,000,000 square miles, it is more than twice the size of the second largest ocean and encompasses a greater area than all of the world's land surfaces combined. It occupies approximately one-third of the total surface of the earth.

The immensity of the Pacific is an inescapable reality; even the swiftest commercial jetliners require fifteen to twenty hours to cross its vast expanse. Although in total there are literally tens of thousands of bits of land rising above the blue waters, ranging in size from continental to minute, these islands occupy but a fraction of the Pacific Basin. Many continent-sized portions of the ocean are completely devoid of islands, without a single piece of land breaking the surface of the water. It is possible to travel great distances in any part of the Pacific except the southwest without coming in sight of land for weeks or even months. Indeed, the first expedition to circumnavigate the globe, that of Magellan in 1520-22, sighted only two small islands while traversing the Pacific from southernmost South America to Guam, in ninety-eight days of sailing.

The Pacific is largely a tropical ocean. Although it extends almost to the Arctic Circle in the north and a few degrees beyond the Antarctic Circle in the south, its greatest girth is in equatorial regions, and most of its islands and sea lanes are within the tropics. Its personality, while not always as placid as its name would indicate, is characterized by such

1

low latitude phenomena as tepid water temperatures, persistent trade winds, towering cumulonimbus clouds, exquisite sunsets, abrupt but short-lived thunderstorms, extensive coral reefs that separate pounding surf from peaceful lagoons, brilliant beaches inevitably bordered by towering palms, and infinitely varied marine life.

The Oceanic Influence

The sea, then, is the one ineluctable fact of this region. Its influence is dominant, and only in the interior of large land masses (Australia, New Guinea, New Zealand) is it possible to escape its pervasiveness. This influence is felt in many ways.

The ocean is a barrier in the basic sense. It prevents the spread of most types of terrestrial life. Only a relatively few varieties of plants and animals can survive a long trip from one land area to another: essentially, those with seeds that are watertight and floatable (as the pandanus); those which can live comfortably in driftwood (as weevils and lizards); those light enough to be wafted long distances by the wind (as fern spores or small spiders); or those which may be carried inadvertently by flying creatures (such as mites on bats or small arthropods on birds). Thus possibilities for natural diffusion across an ocean are limited. So it is that biogeographers give much attention to the possible existence of paleohistorical "land bridges" to explain the distribution patterns of many life forms on Pacific islands. It is much easier to visualize the diffusion of terrestrial life across this ocean if it can be postulated that there were land connections from Southeast Asia to Australia or from South America through Antarctica to the Southwest Pacific.

On the other hand, the ocean serves as a link between lands that are thousands of miles apart. The buoyancy of water enables relatively heavy objects to float for indefinite periods, and the persistence of both ocean and air currents provides a means of locomotion for a floating object. It is for man that the connectivity function of the ocean is most significant. Even with relatively frail craft, he has sailed to the remotest reaches of that 71 per cent of the earth's surface that is aqueous. And where man has gone, he has taken with him plants and animals, both cultigens and parasites, affording further means for diffusion of species. Thus man and his camp followers (such as dog, rat, flea, pig, sweet potato, and taro) have swarmed over the islands of the Pacific, investigating them all and settling on all but the poorest.

Wherever man has settled in the Pacific, the ocean has continued to exercise a dominant influence on his life. It contributes importantly to his economy, both subsistence and commercial, by providing a habitat for food resources. Although tropical waters cannot generally match the great quantity of fish found in certain mid-latitude fisheries, the variety of marine life around Pacific islands is unparalleled. On most Pacific islands, coastal fishing occupies a significant niche in the way of life.

Inter-island communication provides another focus for assessing the influence of the ocean. Trading and raiding, colonization and warfare, exploitation and missionizing: the sea provides an avenue for these and other human interactions. In the past, Tongans sailed to Fiji to learn the art of warfare, New Hebrideans were "blackbirded" to work in Australian sugar cane fields, Pitcairners were resettled in the more permissive environment of Norfolk Island, Hawaii was "unified" by Kamehameha's flotilla of war canoes advancing northwestward from the Big Island. Today, Cook Islanders migrate to New Zealand, Nauruans export phosphate to the world, Japanese tuna boats support the Samoan economy, and overcrowded Gilbert Islanders are resettled in Fiji.

Whereas its roles as barrier, as link, as source of food, and as communication medium are all of major importance, it is likely that the influence of the Pacific Ocean on climate is most significant of all. The physical nature of the Pacific Basin is in large measure determined by the characteristics of the water and their concomitant effects on the overlying air. The southern part of Australia and nearly all of New Zealand are dominated by the westerlies, but no other significantly inhabited area under consideration in this volume is influenced by cool air masses. Most of the Pacific area is dominated by tropical airflow, particularly by the easterly trade winds. These wind systems demonstrate characteristics acquired from the warm waters over which they blow; thus warm, relatively humid conditions are to be expected over most of the region most of the time. Precipitation conditions vary, but in general it is abundant. There is tremendous potential for rainfall, and unstable lapse rates often develop, resulting in very heavy rains, both seasonal and nonperiodic. Thunderstorms are widespread, typhoons are known in some parts of the region, and milder tropical disturbances also occur. Spectacular clouds, thunder, lightning, and rainbows are commonplace. Even on the so-called "desert" islands, which are small coralline outcrops with so little relief and area that they do not trigger air mass uplift and showers, there is an abundance of moisture in the air. In most Pacific island areas, then, land and water and air share the uniform attributes of warmth and moisture.

Land Masses of the Pacific Basin

Despite the vastness of its water surface and the importance of its sea lanes and fisheries, it is not the ocean itself that draws most of our attention; rather, we focus upon the relatively small amount of land that is scattered over the Pacific Basin, for this is where man lives in varying densities and patterns. In keeping with this book's emphasis upon Australasia, we will exclude from consideration the "continental fringe" islands around the margin of the Pacific. The near-coastal islands of the Americas (the Chilean islands, the Galápagos, the offshore Mexican islands, the Channel Islands, the coastal islands of British Columbia and Alaska, and the Aleutians) are more properly considered in conjunction with the countries they border; and the significant islands on the western margin of the Pacific (the Kuriles, Japan, the Ryukyus, Taiwan, the Philippines, and Indonesia) are integral parts of Asia.

The remaining land areas in the Pacific (those that are the subject

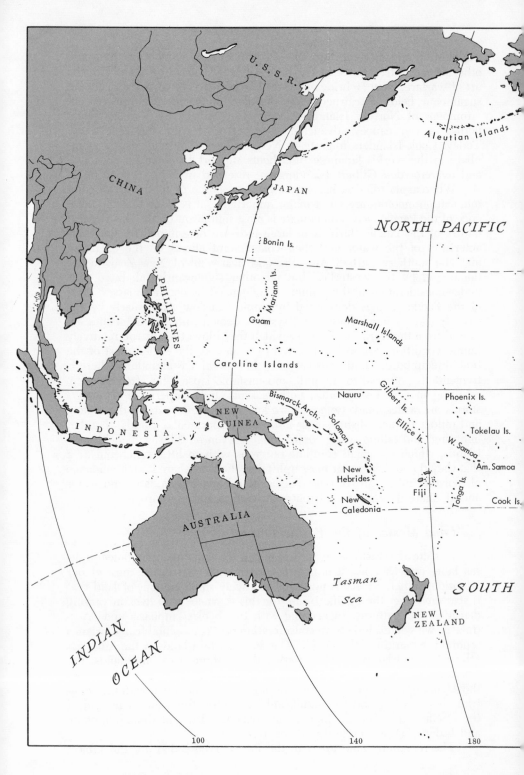

U.S.S.R.

Aleutian Islands

CHINA

JAPAN

NORTH PACIFIC

Bonin Is.

PHILIPPINES

Mariana Is.

Guam

Marshall Islands

Caroline Islands

Nauru

Gilbert Is.

Phoenix Is.

INDONESIA

Bismarck Arch.

NEW
GUINEA

Solomon Is.

Ellice Is.

Tokelau Is.

W. Samoa

Am. Samoa

New
Hebrides

Fiji

Tonga Is.

Cook Is.

New
Caledonia

AUSTRALIA

Tasman
Sea

SOUTH

NEW
ZEALAND

INDIAN

OCEAN

100

140

180

4

Figure 1-1 The Pacific Setting

5

of this volume) consist of a tremendous number of tropical islands, a small continent (Australia) that is basically subtropical in nature but whose low-latitude characteristics are sometimes obscured, and a large island group (New Zealand) that is subtropical only on its northern margin. These land masses are distributed very unevenly throughout the Pacific, with the principal concentration in the southwest portion. Most of the northern part of the ocean, between California and Japan east-west and between the Aleutians and Midway north-south, is absolutely devoid of any land rising above the surface of the sea. An equally extensive expanse of the eastern Pacific, stretching from the west coast of the Western Hemisphere continents to about the 135th meridian (west), is dotted with less than a dozen tiny isles. In its south central and southwestern portions, however, the ocean is peppered with islands.

The northernmost chain of oceanic islands, separated from the other tropical groups by 1,500 miles of empty ocean, is the Hawaiian archipelago. It consists of a 2,000-mile string of islands and reefs that extends westward from the island of Hawaii (at 155° west longitude) to Kure (almost at the 180th meridian). Normally the term Hawaiian Islands is restricted to the easternmost portion of the chain, a group of about two dozen islands of which only four have significant population.

Some two thousand miles west and south of the Hawaiian chain are found the numerous small islands of Micronesia. Almost all are located north of the Equator and west of the international date line. There are four principal groups of islands in Micronesia: the Marianas, the Carolines, the Marshalls, and the Gilberts. Nearly all of the individual islands are coral atolls of quite small size.

Situated east and south of Micronesia, and sprawling across sixty degrees of longitude (mostly east of the 180th meridian) and fifty degrees of latitude (mostly south of the Equator), is the great triangle of Polynesia, with its corners at Hawaii, Easter Island, and New Zealand. Although the vast majority of the islands are small, flat atolls, some are high, rugged, and volcanic. The principal island groups in Polynesia include the Line, Phoenix, Ellice, Tokelau, Samoan, Tongan, Cook, Society, Tuamotu, and Marquesas islands. At the western edge of Polynesia lies the important Fiji group, which has many of the characteristics of both Polynesia and Melanesia.

In the southwestern corner of the Pacific lie the islands of Melanesia, which are separated from Micronesia to the north by an extensive equatorial expanse of island-free ocean and from Polynesia to the east by a similar spread of landless water. Although the majority of the Melanesian islands are small and coralline, the regional landscape is dominated by several dozen "high" islands, whose rugged relief and volcanic origins impart a distinctive character to the land masses of this part of the Pacific. Most notable, of course, is New Guinea, whose area (300,000 square miles) is exceeded by that of only one other island in the world, and whose population (3,000,000) is greater than that of all the other Pacific islands combined. The other important islands of Melanesia include the Bismarck archipelago (New Britain, New Ireland, and the Admiralty Islands), the Solomons, the New Hebrides, and New Caledonia.

A thousand miles to the southeast of New Caledonia, and well beyond the margins of the true tropics, is New Zealand. This southernmost nation in the Eastern Hemisphere consists of two principal islands (named the South and the North), which are the twelfth and fourteenth largest in the world, as well as much smaller Stewart Island in the far south. New Zealand's high relief and generally rugged terrain reflect its location at the confluence of two major submarine mountain arcs, one emanating southeastward from New Guinea and New Caledonia and the other extended southward from Fiji.

The largest land mass of the Pacific area is the continent of Australia, which is approximately the same size as the forty-eight conterminous states of the United States. Situated 1,400 miles northeast of New Zealand, 1,000 miles southwest of New Caledonia, and less than one hundred miles south of New Guinea, Australia is characterized by relatively level terrain and dry climate. Thus its environmental characteristics differ significantly from those of the other land areas of the Pacific Basin.

The Physical Nature of the Islands

Despite the pervading influence of the ocean, there is considerable physical diversity among the islands of the Pacific. This diversity is in large measure the result of variations in relief; thus the most important differences are between the high islands and the low islands. Other significant environmental controls include island structure and lithology (especially coralline versus non-coralline), exposure (windward or leeward), and position with respect to planetary wind circulation patterns (easterlies, westerlies, monsoons).

THE GEOLOGIC FUNDAMENT. The land masses of the Pacific, large and small, can be divided into four essential groups on the basis of their geologic underpinnings, primarily lithology, structure, and areal extent. Although there are notable variations within each group, meaningful generalizations can be made.

Continental Islands. A few of the lands in the region under discussion are vast enough to be divorced from simplistic environmental relationships. They are sufficiently large so that the oceanic influence is not pervasive; their terrain is sufficiently varied so that low latitude location is muted by the harsher effect of altitude; and the resulting environmental diversity renders invalid most broad generalizations. There are four such "continental islands" in Australasia: Australia itself, New Guinea, and the two main islands of New Zealand. Any meaningful understanding of their characteristics requires individual analysis.

High Islands. The "high" islands of the Pacific are typically large in size, varied in relief, and steep of slope. Some are totally of volcanic origin, usually associated with the "Pacific rim of fire," that unstable oceanic perimeter that comprises the Pacific coastal margins of South America, North America, and Asia, and is distinct and conspicuous in the Melanesian portion of Australasia. Others have a less spectacular, if more complex, geologic structure, consisting of a variety of types of bedrock interspersed with igneous intrusions. A number of the volcanoes are still active, but most are extinct, or at least quiescent. Whether active or dormant, however, the influence of vulcanism on the landscape has been significant.

Some of the high islands consist of a single peak rising from the ocean floor, like Mooréa in French Polynesia; others are composed of multiple volcanic peaks, like the Big Island of Hawaii; and still others comprise a range or chain of mountains, as New Caledonia. Whatever the pattern, however, almost all share certain basic characteristics. The slopes are steep and abrupt, the valleys are deep and small, the streams are swift and clear. Mountains, hills, or both make up the bulk of the island area, and coastal plains are either absent or of quite limited extent. Local relief is often spectacular, with peaks rising thousands of feet within only a short distance of the shore. Mountains reach elevations exceeding 6,000 feet on Savaii in Western Samoa, 7,000 feet in Tahiti, 10,000 feet on Bougainville in the Solomons, and 13,000 feet in Hawaii. Mauna Kea on the Big Island of Hawaii is often said to be the world's highest mountain from base to summit, as its peak is nearly 14,000 feet above sea level and its base is some 18,000 feet below sea level on the ocean floor. Even on islands where the peaks reach only 4,000 feet or 5,000 feet in height, clouds persist about the summits much of the time.

Uplifted coral platforms. The occurrence of coralline structures in the Pacific is widespread. Many are in the form of narrow reefs, but some appear as more extensive platforms or amorphous masses. Some such platforms have been uplifted above the surface of the sea, forming islands of small to medium size. The tectonic uplift is sometimes complex and may involve tilting or faulting of the platform. The resulting island is typically low-lying, but its surface form may be irregular and occasionally shows considerable relief. Such islands do not have the physical diversity that characterizes volcanic islands, but most have sufficient variety of terrain to keep the coral platform from having a homogeneous environment. Examples of coral platform islands include Makatéa (in the Tuamotus), Nauru, Tongatapu (in Tonga), and Ocean Island.

Atolls. The most common type of island in the Pacific, by far, is the coral atoll. Atolls are remarkable entities composed of the massed and cemented calcareous skeletons of small anthozoan animals called polyps. These relatively long and narrow coralline structures are normally built in shallow water fringing some island or other land mass. Most atolls are connected in some fashion to volcanic cores of dense basalt, although in many instances the cores are deeply submerged beneath the sea. Diastrophic movements of the earth's crust often raise the coral slightly above sea level, where, in the normal workings of nature over a long period of time, soil may form, vegetation may grow, and a new island may be formed.

As the coral structure is normally begun as an island-fringing feature, even though the island that it initially fringed may subsequently sink beneath the sea, the atoll typically takes a roughly circular form, separating the active waters of the open ocean from the quiet waters of the enclosed lagoon. The term "atoll," in fact, implies a ring-shaped structure. In actuality, the ring is rarely a complete enclosure; rather it consists of a string of closely spaced coral islets (the individual islet is called a "motu"), separated by narrow water passageways.

An atoll is a typical example of a "desert island." It is low-lying (often its highest point is only a few feet above sea level) and flat, narrow and sandy, and in many cases has no surface streams at all. They are special islands that engender special feelings in people familiar with them. In the colorful prose of James Michener:

A coral atoll, circular in form, subtended a shallow lagoon. On the outer edge giant green combers of the Pacific thundered in majestic fury. Inside, the water was blue and calm. Along the shore of the lagoon palm trees bent their towering heads as the wind directed. . . . The world contains certain patterns of beauty that impress the mind forever. . . . The list need not be long, but to be inclusive it must contain a coral atoll with its placid lagoon, the terrifyingly brilliant sands and the outer reef shooting great spires of spindrift a hundred feet into the air. Such a sight is one of the incomparable visual images of the world.[1]

Although the term "atoll" was actually coined to apply to certain islands in the Indian Ocean, the great majority of the world's atolls are in the Pacific. Nearly all of the Micronesian islands, most of the Polynesian islands, and a large share of the Melanesian islands are atolls.

THE FRINGING REEFS. Regardless of type, practically every tropical island in the Pacific is bordered by, or enclosed by, a coral reef.[2] The largest coralline feature in the world is Australia's Great Barrier Reef, which is a semicontinuous complexity of coral islands, reefs, and shoals that extends for some 1,250 miles along the northeastern coast of the continent. Of almost similar magnitude is the fringing reef that encircles the island of New Caledonia.

The ubiquity of reefs associated with the Pacific islands is a reflection of the remarkable fecundity of the coral polyp. Polyps are not actually very hardy creatures; they cannot survive in water that is very cold or very fresh or very dirty, and they cannot live more than a few tens of feet below the surface of the ocean, as they attach themselves to skeletons of preceding generations and extract lime from seawater to build their own shells. But they occur in uncountable billions in the tropical waters of the world, and the structures they construct are massive and sturdy. Accordingly, their contribution to life in the Pacific Basin is incalculable, and their presence in the oceanic landscape is immensely important.

[1] James A. Michener, *Return to Paradise* (New York: Random House, Inc., 1951), pp. 6-7.
[2] Some islands in the eastern Pacific, like the Marquesas, have very restricted reef development, apparently owing to the upwelling of cooler water that is unsuitable for the survival of coral polyps.

The coral polyp is preyed upon by a variety of forms of marine life, particularly echinoderms. In recent years major depredations by certain varieties of starfish on polyps have been recognized, and special concern is being shown for sections of the Great Barrier Reef that have been denuded of polyps by starfish.

FLORISTIC PATTERNS.   The Pacific islands house a remarkable diversity of plant communities, although, for the most part, the number of species is relatively few (except in New Guinea), doubtless due to isolation. A further function of isolation is the large proportion of endemic plants (those found only on one or a small group of islands, and nowhere else in the world). For example, more than 70 per cent of the native floral species of both New Caledonia and Hawaii are endemic. The heavy rainfall of the high islands, combined with the characteristic high temperature and humidity of the tropics, produces an environment that supports a perennially green, almost overpoweringly luxuriant vegetation. The dense vegetation of the rain forest, with its tall trees, multiple canopies, abundance of parasitic growth, and sunless floor, is most widespread in Melanesia, where the extensive mountains of such large islands as New Guinea, New Britain, Bougainville, Guadalcanal, and Espíritu Santo intercept a great deal of precipitation. Smaller areas of rain forest are found on other islands, such as the windward slopes of Viti Levu in Fiji or certain southeastern hillsides on Tutuila in American Samoa, but it is clear that only an optimum combination of elevation and exposure can produce enough rainfall to support a rain forest association.

All is not rain forest in the high islands. Many areas have less luxuriant natural vegetation, due to lower annual rainfall totals or to seasonal dry periods, or both. More open forests occur in many localities, savanna woodlands are found on leeward slopes and protected exposures, and swamp associations occupy many river valleys and coastal plains. Furthermore, fairly extensive grasslands, often man-induced, are developed on some of the larger islands. Grasslands are most notable at middle elevations (4,000 feet–6,000 feet) in New Guinea, where they support the greatest population densities of the island. Another special floristic association in New Guinea is the moss or cloud forest, which is characterized by stunted trees, thick mossy ground cover, and almost continual mist. It occupies fairly extensive areas between about 7,000 feet and 11,000 feet elevation.

The coral islands are so small and low that their vegetation is much sparser. The drier conditions, occasioned by scanty rainfall and porous soil, support a relatively uniform flora of maritime and drought-resistant plants. Apart from the ubiquitous pandanus and coconut palm, and various plants cultivated by the islanders, there is often little more than scattered grasses, bushes, and herbaceous plants. Many of the smaller islands are entirely treeless, and the number of native plant species on an atoll is usually less than two dozen.

Of all the plants of the Pacific Basin, none is more notable or significant than the coconut palm. It is the conspicuous species of the coastal lowlands; the island whose beaches are not fringed with palm trees is a rarity indeed. The extraordinarily widespread occurrence of the coconut palm apparently represents a combination of natural diffusion (the coconut is capable of floating some distance over the ocean, and then lodging on a beach and sprouting) and cultural diffusion (its usefulness is legion, so that natives frequently took coconuts with them on their migrations from one island to another). The principal value of the coconut palm is the food and drink provided by its nut and the commercial copra industry supported by its desiccated meat, but significant use is also made of its wood, its leaves, and even its flowers.

FAUNA OF THE ISLANDS.   There is considerable diversity in the faunal complement of the Pacific islands, as might be expected with habitats ranging from mountainous rain forests to barren, sandy atolls. Overall, however, animal life is notable for its sparsity, particularly with reference to terrestrial forms. The barrier effect of a great ocean severely restricts natural diffusion, so that on most islands the more conspicuous elements of the fauna are species that have been introduced by man.

The greatest abundance and variety of terrestrial animal life is found in New Guinea, with a general decrease in numbers and variety eastward and northward from there. This is logical, considering the apparent spread of most animal life across the Pacific from Southeast Asia and to a lesser extent from Australia. Thus Melanesia has a richer fauna than either Polynesia or Micronesia, and in general the larger islands are more bountifully endowed with animal life than the smaller ones.

Even so, terrestrial mammals are quite limited everywhere. New Guinea has considerable variety, ranging from marsupials and monotremes through rodents to wild dogs and wild pigs; but even there no native primates or ungulates, and very few carnivores, are to be found. On the other islands native terrestrial mammals are very poorly represented and in many cases totally absent.

Man has altered the faunal pattern considerably by introducing exotic animals to the islands. Rats, for example, are now almost ubiquitous throughout the Pacific Basin and serve as a major destroyer of coconuts on many islands. Feral livestock (domesticated animals that have reverted to a wild existence) are also widespread. Feral goats, sheep, pigs, and cattle are prominent on most of the Hawaiian islands, and feral pigs and goats are found in a number of other localities. Exotic wildlife species from other parts of the world have been brought to many Pacific islands. New Zealand, where ungulates from three continents and marsupials from a fourth are widespread, is the prime example; others include New Caledonia's large deer population and the varied ungulates that have been released in Hawaii.

The avian fauna is much richer, of course. An ocean is less of a barrier to birds than to mammals. New Guinea is world-renowned for its remarkably varied bird life, most notably represented by a multitude of species of birds of paradise. The larger Melanesian islands also have considerable variety in their birds, and even small atolls are likely to be well endowed.

Man, again, has played an important role by introducing various species, particularly the Indian mynah, the bulbul, the English sparrow, and the starling, all of which are widespread throughout the Pacific.

Reptiles and amphibians are fairly common in the larger Melanesian islands, particularly New Guinea, but are much less common elsewhere. Insects and other arthropods occur in varying quantity and diversity, once again with the greatest representation in Melanesia. Crabs and other littoral crustaceans are especially numerous throughout the region.

The Peopling of the Pacific Islands

The multiple islands of the Pacific Basin have always been far removed from the mainstream of world consciousness and interest; thus they have not been subjected to a series of major colonizations, invasions, and wars. Even so, the present population of the region is an imperfect amalgam of many diverse groups, who have spread sporadically through the islands, leaving imprints both lasting and ephemeral.

The native peopling of the Pacific islands was accomplished over an exceedingly long period of time, involving numerous groups of migrants who moved out generally but erratically from Southeast Asia across the vast ocean, possibly starting as much as 25,000 years ago. The migratory patterns were varied, complex, and overlapping, and still are understood very imperfectly.

It is believed that Negritos were the first to penetrate the Pacific, certainly as far as the Philippines and New Guinea, and probably into Australia and Micronesia as well. These were small-statured, primitive people, with a subsistence economy and a low level of material culture. Their imprint on the region was small, and they generally were inundated and absorbed by later, more advanced groups. Still, some Negritos exist today in New Guinea, and as late as 1967 government patrols encountered tribesmen who had never before seen either white men or government representatives.

By and large, the Negritoid peoples were inundated by later migrants into the region. Many of the later groups were primarily Negroid in racial characteristics, whereas others were predominantly Caucasoid and still others possessed distinctively Mongoloid features. Racial mixing, then, has taken place on a grand scale over a long period of time, and the combination of hybridization and migration has resulted in a veritable patchwork of racial types across the Pacific. Distinctions are sometimes made among Melanesians, Polynesians, and Micronesians, but any broad generalizations about their ethnic characteristics must be examined with great care.

The various natives were resident in the islands for hundreds or thousands of years before the first Europeans appeared on the scene. For the most part they evolved a communal village life, often extending the concept of "family" beyond blood relationship. They developed a subsistence economy based on gardening and fishing, which are still the basic forms of livelihood for most of the people in the region. Root crops, such as taro and yams, and tree crops, such as breadfruit and coconuts, were then and are now staples in their agriculture.

Penetration by Europeans into the Pacific was slow and sporadic. From the early 1500's, when the first explorations were made, some three centuries elapsed before the European powers began to express serious interest in colonization of the islands. The first century of European exploration, the sixteenth, was primarily an Iberian century, with Portuguese and Spanish ships in the majority. The Portuguese captain Abreu was the first definitely recorded European explorer; his exploration was mostly restricted to coastal New Guinea. Magellan's crew made the first circumnavigation of the globe in the early 1520's, but managed to see less than a half dozen islands. Various other Spanish and Portuguese ships navigated the Pacific during that century, but their records were singularly poor, and many of their discoveries apparently went unrecorded. During the seventeenth century, Dutch explorers were in the ascendancy. The Netherlands established its hegemony in the East Indies, and Dutch navigators traveled widely in the Pacific. The eighteenth century was a time of increasing exploration in the Pacific Basin for ships from many nations; however, the French and British were dominant. The greatest of all Pacific explorers, Captain James Cook, made his three voyages during the 1760's and 1770's.

Following soon after the explorers, the islands were intruded upon by European gatherers and hunters (of sandalwood, pearl shell, whales, and other specialized products) and by traders bartering European goods. Missionaries also made a significant imprint and stimulated production for trade. Thus some Europeans had begun to settle on Pacific islands as early as the sixteenth century; however, the general region did not come under significant European influence until after 1800. From then on, native culture and institutions, as well as the people themselves, began to disappear with appalling and growing rapidity. By the time the nineteenth century ended, most of the native communities into which Europeanization had penetrated had dwindled greatly in numbers. Furthermore, on a number of islands a new population element was introduced when Asian laborers came to work on plantations and in mines.

As late as 1840 practically all of the Pacific islands were unclaimed by European powers, with the exception of Spain's requisition of some of the Marianas. France began to stake claims in the 1840's, but the British government remained uninterested, despite much urging by some groups (especially Australians), until German trading firms began to establish commercial (and colonizing) relations in the Pacific in the 1870's. There then developed a race for control in the Pacific Basin among France, Germany, Great Britain, and to a lesser extent the United States. There were several confrontations of naval strength, particularly focused upon Samoa. Often it seemed that a military crisis was about to erupt in the Pacific, but events such as the Franco-Prussian War, the Boer War, and the Apia (Samoa) hurricane disaster of 1889 distracted the participants.

During the latter part of the nineteenth century, colonial hegemony was established over practically every island or island group in the region.

By the turn of the twentieth century, European or American powers had taken over the Pacific Basin. Germany entered the 1900's as an important colonial power; she controlled Western Samoa, Northeastern New Guinea, the Bismarck archipelago, Nauru, and the principal islands of Micronesia. Britain governed Papua (southeastern New Guinea), the Solomon Islands, Fiji, and a number of minor island groups, and had a protectorate relationship with Tonga. France ruled New Caledonia, the far-flung islands of French Polynesia, and (with Britain) the condominium of the New Hebrides. The principal possessions of the United States were Hawaii, Guam, and eastern Samoa.

Germany was stripped of her overseas possessions during World War I, and Japan made an appearance in the Pacific island scene at this time when German Micronesia was given in mandate to her. Western Samoa was mandated to New Zealand, northwestern New Guinea and the Bismarcks went to Britain and Australia jointly, and Nauru was made a cumbersome triple mandate of Britain, New Zealand, and Australia.

World War II brought abrupt and lasting changes to the Pacific islands. Moving from secret bastions in Micronesia (which had been closed to the outside world since the mid-thirties) and her invading spearheads in the East Indies and the Philippines, Japanese military might quickly overran about half of Melanesia. A lengthy series of bloody battles was fought in New Guinea and the Solomons, and air and sea attacks spread devastation in the Bismarck archipelago and throughout Micronesia. Although most of Polynesia was spared direct battle damage, it shared with Melanesia and Micronesia the significant economic and social repercussions that go with three and a half years of adjacency to a major region of warfare. Stone Age Melanesians, simplistic Micronesians, and placid Polynesians were jerked abruptly into the international realities of the atomic age, and the South Pacific has never been the same since. Native standards and values were rapidly abandoned or significantly modified, a cash economy did away with the last vestiges of a barter system, material possessions from the Western world achieved great desirability, transportation and communication networks were vastly improved. For the first time, solid feelings about colonialism and nationalism began to develop, though at a slower rate and on a smaller scale than in most other parts of the underdeveloped world.

Economically, the Pacific islands enjoyed a general period of prosperity in the immediate postwar years. Private enterprise was officially discouraged at first, largely because the major colonial powers had socialist-trending governments in power. The pendulum soon swung the other way, however, and private investment was strongly encouraged. For a few years after the war most of the islands reaped the benefits of high prices for their primary produce—copra, cocoa, coffee, sugar, rubber— but later the price structures leveled out, and virtually all of the island groups reinforced their prewar economic position of being financial drains upon the colonial powers.

In more recent years, the winds of political, social, and economic change have been freshening. Western Samoa and Nauru have become independent, Hawaii has become a state, and various islands (such as New Caledonia and Fiji) have been granted larger measures of internal self-government. Social stratification and ethnic discrimination have been diminished; one man-one vote democracy has been disseminated to even the most backward tribes of Papua, Cook Islanders can migrate freely to New Zealand, and Tahitians have the same French legal perquisites as Parisians. The economy of the islands still must contend with the triple handicaps of limited resources, lack of capital, and remoteness from world markets; but even in this sphere changes can be noted. Although copra, which must be marketed in competition with much greater volumes of production from other tropical areas, remains the cornerstone of the regional economy, diversity is making itself felt. Burgeoning markets in Japan and to a lesser extent in New Zealand provide outlets for bananas and sugar from various islands, New Guinea coffee is sold increasingly in Australia, expanding supplies of minerals are marketed from New Caledonia, and commercial fisheries have become a mainstay of the Samoan economy.

With the twentieth century more than two-thirds past, perhaps the most far-reaching continuing development in the Pacific Basin is the improvement and expansion of transportation patterns and the concomitant accelerated growth of tourism. Signaled by the achievement of statehood by Hawaii in 1959 and the building of a jet runway across Tahiti's northwestern lagoon in 1960, the world has discovered the Pacific. Tourist travel to Hawaii grew from 185,000 in 1958 to 875,000 in 1967, and is expected to reach 2,000,000 by 1975. The traditional route southwest from Hawaii to Australia-New Zealand with a stopover in Fiji is still the principal throughway of the South Pacific, but there are now frequent jet stops at Tahiti, Samoa, and New Caledonia as well. More than twenty scheduled airlines serve the islands (exclusive of Hawaii), and such previously inaccessible localities as Bora-Bora, Guam, Tonga, Port Moresby, and Rabaul are on the verge of tourist inundation.

Contemporary Ethnic Diversity

The present population of the Pacific islands is about 4,500,000. (This total does not include Australia and New Zealand, which will be discussed later, or the western half of the island of New Guinea, which is part of Indonesia and will not be considered in this book.) Roughly 80 per cent of this number represents indigenous people (including mixed bloods), and of the remaining 20 per cent, about two-thirds are Asian and one-third are European. Of the natives, more than 80 per cent is Melanesian (including Papuan), and the remainder is about two-thirds Polynesian and one-third Micronesian.

The natives generally occupy their traditional areas:

1. Negritos are restricted to remote highland areas of New Guinea.
2. The Melanesians normally live in small village communities, each of which is relatively independent and self-contained, and usually led by a headman

rather than a chief. As a generalization it can be said that coastal-dwelling Melanesians tend to be more advanced socially and economically than those who reside in the interior, and that Fijians are far advanced over most other Melanesian groups.

3. Micronesians characteristically inhabit small coastal villages. Considerable differences can be noted from island to island in Micronesia.

4. Polynesians are quite diverse, as might be expected from their wide diffusion over the Pacific.

Natives comprise the great majority of the population in most islands and island groups. Such a statement does not take into consideration the mixed bloods, as there are no accurate data on their proportion in the total population. As a rule of thumb it can be stated that the percentage of mixed bloods is quite significant in much of Polynesia, much less notable in Micronesia, and not important at all in Melanesia. The only major localities where natives are not in the majority are Hawaii, Fiji, and New Caledonia.

The Hawaiian islands comprise one of the great population melting pots of the world. The native population is fast disappearing and represents but a small fraction of the total, although part-Hawaiians make up about as large a proportion (16 per cent) of the whole as North Americans do. The largest element of the population is Japanese (one-third of the total); other significant groups include Filipinos, Chinese, and Portuguese. Intermarriage among the various groups continues to increase.

The population of Fiji represents a unique case in the Pacific. Its total population of more than half a million is less than 40 per cent native Fijian and more than 50 per cent Indian. The latter are descendants of indentured laborers brought in to work the sugar cane fields two or three generations ago. The extremely contrasting cultures of these two groups, combined with the rapid birth rate of both, presents increasingly difficult problems each year.

The situation in New Caledonia is different still. Its population of less than 100,000 includes approximately equal numbers of Melanesians (mostly New Caledonians) and Europeans (largely French), which combine to form about seven-eighths of the total. The remainder consists of Asiatics, most of whom are either Vietnamese or Javanese descended from indentured workers imported in the past.

Apart from the three situations just described, non-native peoples comprise only a small minority of the population. Europeans are found in limited numbers, primarily in the larger towns of such islands as Tahiti, American Samoa, New Guinea, and Guam. Orientals occur in a more disseminated pattern. Chinese, for example, are a small but significant minority on many islands, especially in French Polynesia. Vietnamese are also notable on several French islands. Many Japanese migrated to Micronesia during the 1920's and 1930's, but most have now returned to their homeland, and only a scattered few remain.

The population density varies significantly from island to island, following no predictable pattern. In general the greatest densities occur in groups of small islands, such as the Tuamotus or the Ellices. The greatest absolute densities of the entire Pacific Basin are found in the tiny phosphate-producing islands, of which Nauru and Ocean Island are the prime examples. New Guinea, despite its large total population, has a relatively low population density.

The great majority of the peoples of the Pacific islands live in a rural environment, normally in small agricultural or fishing villages. These hamlets are often discrete entities, functionally remote from neighboring villages that may be only a very few miles distant. Frequently the cultural patterns vary significantly from village to village, and sometimes mutually incomprehensible dialects are spoken in neighboring valleys. True urban development is quite limited, and there is a notable scarcity of cities. Apart from Honolulu (with a population exceeding 500,000) there is no real metropolitan center in the region. The largest towns and their approximate 1970 populations are Suva in Fiji (60,000), Noumea in New Caledonia (45,000), Port Moresby in New Guinea (45,000), Hilo on the Big Island of Hawaii (35,000), Apia in Western Samoa (30,000), and Papeete in Tahiti (25,000).

The Islands in Brief

MELANESIA. The *Territory of Papua and New Guinea* is a rather complex political unit administered as an external territory of Australia. It includes the southeastern portion of the island of New Guinea (officially called the Territory of Papua), the northeastern portion of the island of New Guinea, the Bismarck archipelago (of which the largest islands are New Britain, New Ireland, and Manus), and the northern part of the Solomon Islands (primarily Bougainville Island). These rugged, rainy, tropical lands provide homes for more than two million culturally diverse natives. Their economy runs the gamut from primitive, wandering Negrito hunters to sophisticated, urban-dwelling commercial farmers; their social organization varies from fragmented, patrilineal societies in the New Guinea highlands to tightly organized and densely settled matrilineal groups in the coastlands of New Britain. This is one of the most complicated linguistic areas in the world, with more than 500 languages and dialects spoken. The vast majority of the people live in small villages and practice a shifting garden type of subsistence farming. There is an increasing amount of commercial farming, some in small native holdings and some in medium-sized, European-owned plantations. Copra is the principal product, amounting to about half of the territory's total export value; other significant commercial crops include coffee, cocoa, and rubber. Timber and gold are the principal nonagricultural products. Civilization is coming rapidly to the fringe areas of New Guinea; an elected House of Assembly was seated for the first time in 1964, a university was opened in Port Moresby in 1967, and complete political self-determination is anticipated in the near future.

The *British Solomon Islands Protectorate* consists of ten high islands extending in a double chain for nearly 1,000 miles southeast of Bougainville, plus four smaller, nearby island groups. The islands are physically much like those of the Bismarck archipelago, and the native economy is much like that of New Guinea, with village-oriented subsistence gardening as the main activity. The people, however, are not nearly as variegated, either physically or culturally, as the New Guineans, being of basic Melanesian stock and having fewer languages. The commercial economy is quite limited and is essentially based on copra production.

The *New Hebrides* is a condominium administered jointly by France and Great Britain. Some eighty islands, most of them small, are included in the colony, whose total population is about 70,000. The condominium was established in the 1880's, and the two governing powers still maintain duplicate facilities for all governmental functions. Most of the natives are subsistence farmers, although more than half of the copra output (the only important agricultural export) is from native holdings. Recent development of manganese deposits on Efate, the most important island in the group, has given a needed fillip to the economy.

New Caledonia, third largest island in Oceania, is different both physically and culturally from the other high islands of Melanesia. Its mountainous backbone provides a rain shadow effect on the southwestern side, resulting in large areas of scrubby woodland and open savanna, rather than forest. The many valuable mineral deposits of the island—primarily nickel, but also iron and chrome ores—have provided an economic stimulus that has attracted large numbers of French settlers, so that the native population is no longer numerically dominant. Indeed, the natives live mostly on reserves, where they practice subsistence gardening, or in housing areas set aside for plantation and mine workers. Cattle ranches and coffee plantations are notable rural features, whereas the principal focal point of this French Overseas Territory is the capital city of Noumea, with its fine harbor, huge smelter, and beach resorts.

MICRONESIA. *Nauru*, a single island of only eight and one-half square miles and some 6,000 population, is the smallest independent country in the world, having achieved independence in 1968. The people live on a fertile coastal fringe, but it is the central plateau of the island that supports the economy, for more than 1,500,000 tons of phosphate rock are exported annually.

The *United States Trust Territory of the Pacific Islands* consists of more than 2,000 small islands scattered over twenty degrees of latitude north of the Equator and forty degrees of longitude west of the international date line. Included within this political unit are the Mariana, Caroline, and Marshall Islands, which were German territories until World War I and then became Japanese mandates until the end of World War II. The total land area of the Trust Territory is about the same as that of the island of Oahu in Hawaii. Most of the 90,000 inhabitants depend upon subsistence agriculture and fishing for their livelihood. The principal source of cash income is exported copra.

Guam, although physically a part of the Mariana group, has been a separate United States territory since it was obtained from Spain in 1898.

It is the largest island in all Micronesia and has almost as great a population as the entire Trust Territory. Postwar change has influenced Guam far more than any other part of Micronesia; nearly one-third of the island's area is used by the military and more than one-third of the island's population is from the United States mainland, principally military personnel and dependents. Wages and living standards have risen and most Guamanians now work for either the military or the civilian government. Much emphasis, however, has been put on a diversified "back to the land" movement, so far with indifferent success.

The *Bonin Islands* are former Japanese possessions administered by the United States since World War II and likely to be returned to Japanese rule in the near future. There are about 100 tiny islands in the group, with a total population of less than 9,000.

The *Gilbert and Ellice Islands* constitute a British Crown Colony that consists of thirty-seven small islands (sixteen in the Gilberts, nine in the Ellices, and twelve scattered) extending from Micronesia (the Gilberts) into Polynesia (the Ellices). These are poor and isolated islands, with phosphate (from Ocean Island) and copra as the only important sources of income. The 50,000 people of the colony have long suffered from overcrowding, and there are continuing efforts to resettle some of them elsewhere in the Pacific.

POLYNESIA. *Hawaii*, the newest state of the United States, is comprised of eight principal islands, which rise above the ocean as the summit peaks of a chain of submarine volcanic mountains. These are the most northeasterly islands of the Pacific Basin. Despite their mountainous origin, the islands contain fairly extensive stretches of relatively flat land, and agricultural possibilities are good in many places. The major crops are sugar cane and pineapple, and much area is devoted to the raising of beef cattle. The mainstays of the economy, however, are income derived from tourism and from governmental (especially military) expenditures. The rapidly growing population now numbers about 750,000, with 80 per cent of the people living in the urban environment of metropolitan Honolulu. Hawaii is the principal way station for travel across the Pacific. Both the harbor and the airport of Honolulu are the busiest in the region.

The *Line Islands* consist of eleven transequatorial atolls strung out between Hawaii and French Polynesia. Some are British and some are American, but all are now uninhabited.

The *Overseas Territory of French Polynesia* includes five archipelagos of some 130 islands scattered over twenty-two degrees of latitude and twenty-five degrees of longitude in the Southern Hemisphere. The larger islands are high and volcanic, but the greater number are small atolls. More than half of the total population of some 90,000 lives on the island of Tahiti; the remainder is widely dispersed. The people are primarily subsistence gardeners and fishermen. The three principal exports are phosphate (entirely from Makatéa Island in the Tuamotu archipelago), copra, and vanilla. During the past decade tourism has become the dominant element in the economy, although its influence is restricted almost entirely to

Tahiti, Mooréa, and Bora-Bora. French government expenditures have also increased significantly in recent years, particularly for nuclear testing and experimentation.

Easter Island is a Chilean possession situated in splendid isolation in the southeastern quarter of the Pacific Ocean. It is an island of great archeological renown because of its huge stone statues and tragic history due to slavery and disease. Its population of more than 1,000 engages in subsistence farming and fishing, and raises sheep for export.

The *Tokelau Islands* make up a New Zealand possession located north of Samoa. There are three multiple atolls, providing homes for some 2,000 people, all of whom are Polynesians. Subsistence farming and fishing dominate, and there is some production of copra for sale.

Western Samoa became an independent country in 1962. Consisting of two large and seven small islands, the group has a population of about 140,000. The people live in small coastal villages, which are often located at stream mouths. Apia is the only town of any size. Land holdings are typically communal, and, in addition to a variety of subsistence crops, commercial production is about equally divided among copra, bananas, and cocoa.

In *American Samoa* about 25,000 people inhabit seven islands, but the bulk of the population is on the island of Tutuila. The population total has remained relatively static in recent years, as there is considerable continuing migration to the United States, particularly Hawaii and California. Pago Pago (pronounced "Pango Pango") is the administrative center and has perhaps the best harbor in the entire Pacific Basin. The people live in small coastal villages, raising subsistence crops and producing copra. The catching and canning of tuna has become the leading element of the economy, although tourism is increasing rapidly.

The *Cook Islands* comprise a self-governing territory associated with New Zealand. Located southeast of Samoa, there are fifteen scattered islands, in two general groupings. The southern group is mostly mountainous and relatively fertile; the northern group consists of atolls. Rarotonga is the largest and most important island, with about half of the territory's population of 20,000. A variety of tropical and subtropical crops is raised, in addition to the usual coconuts, and oranges comprise the principal export, to New Zealand.

The *Kingdom of Tonga* is a constitutional monarchy that has been under the protection of Britain since the turn of the century. It includes about 150 islands (a mixture of high volcanic, uplifted coral platform, and low coralline), which are arranged in three more or less discrete groups and spread over 250 miles of ocean. The social structure of the country has been dominated by a royalty-nobility-peasantry orientation, combined with the very strong influence of the Methodist Church. All land is owned by the crown or by certain noble families, but each adult male is given an allotment to use, provided he follows certain planning regulations. The people live in agricultural or fishing villages and are mostly engaged in subsistence activities, although copra, bananas, and watermelons are exported. The economy is mildly flourishing, and there is no public debt; Tonga can be considered a prosperous country by

Pacific standards. About half of the 80,000 Tongans live on the principal island of Tongatapu.

The British Crown Colony of *Fiji*, located on the periphery of both Polynesia and Melanesia, is the principal transportation nexus of the South Pacific. The native Fijians are, from an ethnic standpoint, distinctly Melanesian, although with some differentiating physical characteristics; but their culture is much more strongly Polynesian than Melanesian. In any event, the large admixture of Indians (previously discussed) and the small but significant minorities of Europeans, Chinese, Polynesians, and Micronesians give to Fiji a set of social problems completely unique to the Pacific Basin. There are some 320 islands in the group, of which fewer than one-third are inhabited. More than 85 per cent of the half million inhabitants of the colony live on the two large islands, Viti Levu and Vanua Levu. There is a marked contrast between the windward (south-eastern) and leeward (northwestern) sides of the main islands; the former receive abundant rainfall, support dense forests, and are the favored areas for native settlement, with their village-oriented sub-sistence agriculture. The latter get much less rainfall, are mostly un-forested, and are inhabited largely by Indian sugar cane farmers. Sugar is by far the principal export of the colony, although the profit margin is small; other commercial products include copra, bananas, gold, and lumber. Fiji faces many economic and social problems in the near future, but its economy is bolstered by rapidly increasing tourism.

Focus on the Antipodes

The many islands of the Pacific are closely tied to the various colonial powers—the United States, the United Kingdom, France, Chile, Australia, and New Zealand—who administer them, but in addition, most of them have special relationships with the latter two countries. New Zealand and particularly Australia are the only economically advanced countries in the Pacific Basin, and as such they are in a position to offer much to the islands. They provide markets for island produce; they are a source of capital for island development; they supply manufactured goods to the island consumers; they have a reservoir of technical and managerial talent that the islanders can call upon; they provide services (ranging from currency to health) to the islands; they have accessible boarding schools to which island children can be sent; they comprise an increasing source of tourist expenditure to bolster the economy of the islands; and they anchor one end of an increasingly busy trans-Pacific transportation route that gives some of the islands important stopover business.

Economic, social, and political development will continue in the Pacific, regardless of what happens in Australia and New Zealand. How-ever, the continuing dynamism of the lands Down Under will be reflected to a reduced degree in the Pacific islands, so that progress in Australia and New Zealand will engender progress in the islands.

With this Pacific setting as background, we will now turn our atten-tion to the Anzac nations, considering Australia in some detail.

CHA**2**TER *the unique land*

Australia is the smallest of the world's seven continents and the only one that is comprised of a single political unit. With an area of 2,971,081 square miles, it ranks as the sixth largest country in the world. It occupies an essentially transitional position between the low and middle latitudes, almost 40 per cent of its area being within the tropics. Thus its physical characteristics are reflective of a large, relatively compact land mass in the subtropics, although the great extent of aridity and the concentration of population in the least tropical portions of the country tend to de-emphasize this subtropicality. Australia's greatest poleward extent is the southern end of the island of Tasmania, which reaches beyond 43° south latitude, roughly as far from the Equator as Boston, Buffalo, or Detroit.

Whereas there is nothing remarkable about the geographical position or dimensions of Australia, most other aspects of its physical geography have unusual characteristics that tend to set it apart from the other continents in a variety of ways. The other five inhabited continents exhibit a certain regularity in patterns of physical geography, which give them an element of uniformity and predictability. Generally, position on the continent (encompassing both latitude and nearness to the coast) and various broad distribution patterns of climate, soils, natural vegetation, and native animal life are associated. The persistence of these environmental patterns from continent to continent is a notable feature of the physical geography of the world. In Australia, however, the patterns are interrupted, re-arranged, and otherwise modified.

The Shape of the Land

The general shape of continental Australia can be likened to an east-west oriented football that has been severely constricted on its mid-southern and northeastern margins. The Great Australian Bight comprises an enormous, but relatively shallow, embayment in the southern coast, and the Gulf of Carpentaria makes a smaller but sharper recess in the northeast (Figure 2-1). Apart from these two major indentations, the coastline is fairly smooth and regular in gross outline, although there are many minor irregularities. Islands occur in varying profusion around the margins of the continent, but most of them are quite small. Most important by far is the island state of Tasmania in the southeast, which is twenty-fifth in size among the islands of the world. Other significant islands include King Island and the Furneaux Group in Bass Strait between Tasmania and the mainland, Kangaroo Island off the coast of South Australia, Melville and Bathurst islands off the mid-north coast, several groups in the Gulf of Carpentaria (Groote Eylandt, the Sir Edward Pellew Group, and the Wellesley Islands), the Torres Strait Islands off the northern tip of Queensland, and the varied islands and islets associated with the Great Barrier Reef.

Probably the most important basic generalization about the Australian lithosphere is that the continent is an ancient and stable one. Throughout eons of geologic time it has demonstrated the sort of long-range stability that characterizes the better-known "shield" areas of the Northern Hemisphere (Laurentian, Fenno-scandian, Angara). That is to say, for the most part, major crustal movements have been rare, both vulcanism and diastrophism have been conspicuous by their absence, and the relative position of sea level has not fluctuated with much frequency. Much of the present Australian continent, then, has been in a quiescent, rigid, subaerial situation for millions of years, and this condition has had a marked effect upon the landscape.

In a very real sense Australia is one of the oldest of the continents. It has been subjected to lengthy, relatively uninterrupted periods of weathering and erosion that have subdued its highlands and reduced its surface to one of low elevation and relief. Spectacular topographic features are rare. Only around the margins, particularly in the east, and in a few scattered localities in the interior has there been significant recent orogenic activity resulting in notable mountains. For the most part Australia is replete with desert landforms. Such features as massive knobs and monoliths and domes with exfoliated surfaces, intermittent stream beds, basins of interior drainage with playas, sand plains, and gravel (gibber) plains are characteristic.

THE EASTERN HIGHLANDS.   Extending the entire length of extreme eastern Australia, from northern Queensland to southern Tasmania, is the subdued cordillera of the Eastern Highlands, often referred to as the Great Dividing Range (Figure 2-2A). The highlands had a moderately complex origin, involving a mixture of folding, faulting, warping, igneous intrusions, and limited volcanic extrusions, with the majority of the mountain building activity occurring in late Tertiary time. Most of the highest peaks consist of intruded and uplifted granite masses.

The topographic variety encompassed in the cordillera is easily the

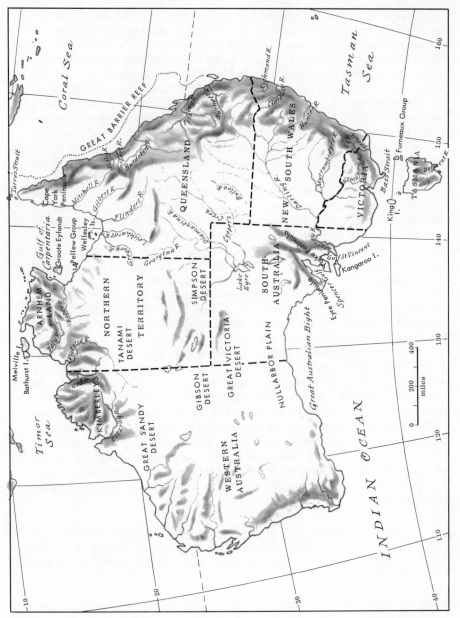

Figure 2-1 Major Physical Features

greatest in Australia. In many places, particularly toward the north, the mountains are so low and subdued that they are quite inconspicuous. In other localities there are massive escarpments, deep gorges, and sheer cliffs that almost defy penetration. On the eastern margin many of the highland ridges project to the sea, descending steeply to the water's edge; however, in most areas there is a narrow fringe of flattish coastland made up of a series of small river valleys, but nowhere of large enough size to be thought of as a coastal plain.

In Queensland the highlands are mostly of low or moderate height, the crests averaging between 2,000 and 3,000 feet above sea level; but in some places the highland area is quite broad. There are some conspicuous peaks and scarps, but mostly low hills are typical. On the eastern side the highlands are interlaced with relatively small, flattish riverine plains, whereas on the west there is a gradual merger with the lowlands of the interior.

In New South Wales the highland is somewhat more restricted in area, but there is a general increase in elevation, relief, and diversity of landforms. The Northern Tablelands are separated from the coast by an irregular but remarkably steep and abrupt escarpment, which is one of the most spectacular terrain features in Australia. In the central portion of the New South Wales highlands is the maze of the Blue Mountains, whose characteristically flat valleys and ridge tops are separated by steeply plunging slopes. In southernmost New South Wales the highland mass reaches its greatest heights, with the Australian Alps extending into Victoria. True alpine terrain is lacking, but an uplifted and eroded table-land presents certain spectacular aspects.

In Victoria the highlands trend to the west with considerable grandeur, encompassing some of the wildest and least accessible terrain on the continent. In the central part of the state the ranges become more subdued, often little more than dissected cuestas, finally terminating near the South Australian border in a discrete highland called the Grampians.

Tasmania contains much topographic variety but is geologically related to, and should be considered part of, the Eastern Highlands. In general, the island represents an uplifted dome that has been dissected and glaciated in its higher parts. Although its relief is restricted, Tasmania is comprised of a complexity of hills and mountains, with limited areas of flat land.

THE CENTRAL PLAINS. West of the highlands there is a gradual transition from hills to plain, as well as a continuing decline in elevation; thus the Eastern Highlands merge more or less imperceptibly with the Central Plains. This region is comprised of an extensive area of lowland, roughly extending north-south from the Gulf of Carpentaria to the Great Bight, and displaced eastward from the center of the continent.

The plains are underlain generally by horizontal sedimentary rocks, with a considerable veneer of more recent alluvial and aeolian deposits on the surface. The lowland is broken in various places by ranges of low, rocky hills, none of which are very extensive in area. Loose deposits of

Landforms

Kimberleys
Hammersley
Ranges
Petermann
Ranges
Macdonnell
Ranges
WESTERN
CENTRAL
PLATEAU
PLAINS
Darling Scarp
Musgrave
Ranges
Flinders Ranges
Mt. Lofty
Ranges
Blue Mts.
SOUTHERN
FAULTLANDS
Alps
Grampians
EASTERN HIGHLANDS

Climate

MONSOONAL
NORTH
ARID INTERIOR
HUMID
EAST
COAST
MEDITERRANEAN
SOUTHWEST
TASMANIA

Artesian Basins

GREAT
ARTESIAN
BASIN

26

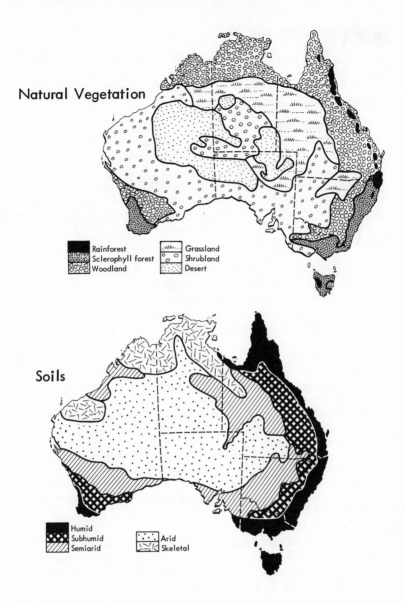

Natural Vegetation

	Rainforest		Grassland
	Sclerophyll forest		Shrubland
	Woodland		Desert

Soils

	Humid		Arid
	Subhumid		Skeletal
	Semiarid		

Figure 2-2 Major Natural Regions

sand are found in many localities, with a very expansive region of lengthy sand ridges in the southeastern corner of the Northern Territory (Simpson Desert) and smaller areas of similar development in the northeastern portion of South Australia.

THE SOUTHERN FAULTLANDS.   A relatively small portion of the continent, located along and near the coast of South Australia, is dominated by a parallel series of steep hills and oceanic gulfs. These are the products of complex crustal movements, primarily faulting along parallel zones of weakness, but including some complicated folding in the north. From west to east are found the varying terrain of the Eyre Peninsula, the rift valley of Spencer Gulf, the hills of Yorke Peninsula, Gulf St. Vincent, and the Mount Lofty Ranges, which merge with the higher and ruggeder Flinders Ranges to the north.

THE WESTERN PLATEAU.   Almost half of the entire continent consists of a rigid pre-Cambrian shield, surface expression of which is a low plateau. Scattered and isolated mountain ranges and higher plateau blocks interrupt the continuity of the surface, but only in three areas has there been general uplift above the plateau.

1. The highest elevations are found in the Pilbara country of the northwestern "shoulder" of Western Australia, where the Hamersley Ranges have peaks that reach to 4,000 feet above sea level. This is broken sandstone country cut by several major river valleys.
2. The Kimberleys district, in the north of Western Australia, consists of a number of confused ranges, mostly composed of rugged sandstone. Although the elevations are not high (peaks up to 3,000 feet), much of the landscape is spectacularly irregular and dissected by deep gorges.
3. The uplands of Arnhem Land, in the far north of the Northern Territory, are lower and less rugged than the two areas just discussed. Nevertheless, the terrain rises above the fringing plains and is characterized by broad, incised river valleys.

There are a number of other rocky ranges in the west, but they are relatively minor features that rise like elongated islands out of the general lowland. Most notable are the Macdonnell, Musgrave, and Petermann ranges in the heart of the continent. These are composed largely of granitic and metamorphic rocks uplifted in an east-west orientation. Antecedent streams draining the ranges often cut directly through the ridges in steep, narrow gorges, which divide the ranges into relatively small blocks.

Impressive, isolated eminences rise above the general plateau level in various places. They are usually rounded granite or sandstone projections with conspicuous exfoliation. The most spectacular are found in the southwestern corner of the Northern Territory, in the form of gigantic monoliths; Ayers Rock is the most famous, but nearby Mount Olga and Mount Conner are equally dramatic.

Almost all of the Western Plateau is arid or semiarid, with the result that mechanical weathering, the fretting action of wind-driven rock particles, and an abundance of loose sand are much in evidence. Extensive portions of the four principal deserts (Tanami, Great Sandy, Gibson, and Great Victoria) are covered with large numbers of parallel, longitudinal dunes, partly stabilized by vegetation.

The Nullarbor Plain is a vast, unusual area with an almost unbelievably flat and smooth surface. It is underlain by limestone and is characterized by an almost complete lack of surface drainage. Unlike the other dry lands of Australia, the Nullarbor Plain has no dry stream courses or intermittent lake beds.

The margin of the plateau slopes gently down to the sea in some places, as in the shoreward portion of the Great Sandy Desert. More common, however, is the presence of a rather abrupt escarpment separating the plateau proper from a fringing coastal plain. This type of development is particularly noticeable in the Nullarbor Plain in the south and along the Darling Scarp in the southwest. There is a narrow but continuous coastal plain along the western edge of Western Australia south of the Kimberleys.

Arid, with Fringes

The relatively undistinguished topography of Australia has an important, if negative, influence on the climate. The general lack of topographic diversity gives rise to broad uniformity of climate, with the result that climatic variation is gradual and transitional over most of the continent, and abrupt areal differences are very limited.

Even so, the basic fact about the Australian climate—its aridity—is in large measure occasioned by a fundamental topographic relationship, the position of the Eastern Highlands. Although we have already noted that this cordillera is neither high nor broad, its north-south orientation is athwart the prevailing easterly winds, thus effectively shutting out moist Pacific air masses from the bulk of the continent. This is by no means the only cause of Australia's expansive aridity, but it is a major one.

Apart from lack of moisture, the most notable feature of the Australian climate is its subtropicality. The latitudinal location assures that high temperatures will be more common than low ones, that seasonal temperature differences will be minimized rather than emphasized, and that diurnal temperature fluctuations are often more meaningful than annual variations.

Thus Australia is a land of clear skies, sunshine, warmth, and little rain. Whereas such a generalization is grossly accurate, it is only an introduction to climatic veracity, an introduction that is best elaborated by consideration of the pattern of climatic regions (Figure 2-2B).

THE ARID INTERIOR. The most extensive climatic region is the vast desert and semi-desert that occupies all of the interior and much of the west of the continent. Well over half of the country receives less than an average fifteen inches of rainfall annually, and on account of a high rate of evaporation, desert conditions are widely prevalent. Rains are few and unpredictable, but often violent and showery when they do occur. Prolonged drought is an omnipresent menace, and it is not uncommon for several years of below-normal precipitation to afflict a large portion of the region. On the other hand, flooding is occasionally experienced, when widespread thunderstorms yield short periods of heavy rain.

This is a subtropical desert region, with warm weather dominant. Summer is likely to be scorchingly hot; maximum temperatures in the nineties, or higher, are to be expected for many weeks over most of the region. Rapid radiational cooling usually permits a decrease of twenty to twenty-five degrees at night, but nocturnal relief is short-lived, and temperatures begin to climb again at sunrise. Gusty winds, blowing sand, and persistent flies add to the unpleasantness of summer.

Winter is characterized by long stretches of pleasant weather, with clear skies, bright sunshine, and mild temperatures (maxima typically in the seventies). Nocturnal cooling often brings midwinter minimum temperatures down into the forties, and mild freezes are not unknown.

THE MOONSOONAL NORTH. The climate of Australia's far north is dominated by the reversing seasonal regime of the monsoon. During four or five months of midsummer there are persistent oceanic (northerly) winds that bring abundant moisture, thunderstorms, and various tropical disturbances onto the continent. For the remainder of the year, high pressure conditions develop over the land, and outblowing (southerly) air flow more or less completely inhibits precipitation. This monsoonal regime is well developed in the Cape York Peninsula, Arnhem Land, and the Kimberleys district, and monsoonal tendencies may extend another two or three hundred miles southward.

"Summer" is only slightly warmer than "winter" in the monsoonal north, but the former's appreciably higher humidity raises the sensible temperatures to an uncomfortable level. The summer monsoon is not a time of continual rainfall; rather there are frequent heavy showers interspersed with long periods of sunshine. Most of the monsoonal region receives from seven to twenty inches of rain during the wettest month, in comparison with an annual total that varies from about twenty-five to sixty inches. The wet season is a time of decreased activity throughout the region; heavy rain combines with flat land to produce widespread conditions of flooding and persistent muddiness, which severely limit transportation.

The dry season is longer than the wet, and is characterized by mild to warm temperatures and generally pleasant weather conditions. Rain is not unknown, but is decidedly rare. As the vegetation dries out, the probability of bush fires increases, and the latter part of the dry season is notable for an almost continual pall of smoke somewhere on the horizon.

THE HUMID EAST COAST. The eastern and southeastern littoral zone of Australia is the region occupied by most of the population, and it is more than just coincidence that this is also a region with relatively abundant rainfall that is well distributed seasonally and reasonably dependable from year to year. The great latitudinal extent of the region encompasses a variation from true tropical conditions in northern Queensland to a mid-latitude condition in southern Victoria. Thus, temperature variations are minimal in the north, but there are major seasonal differences in the south.

Rainfall totals vary from as little as twenty inches in sheltered locations to more than one hundred inches in a few exposed hillside sites. In general, it can be said that precipitation ranges from adequate to super-abundant. Summer is the rainy season in the north, winter is the time of maximum precipitation in the south, and the regime is well balanced in the center. Even in this well-watered environment, however, droughts occasionally occur.

THE MEDITERRANEAN SOUTHWEST. In the two southwest corners of Australia—one area centering on Perth in Western Australia and the other focussing on Adelaide in South Australia—there is a distinctive development of "mediterranean" type climate. This is a subtropical dry summer situation, distinguished by its inverted precipitation regime; winter is the wet season, whereas summer is almost rainless.

Indeed, summer is almost desert-like in its characteristics, except in the immediate vicinity of the coast. Temperatures are high during the day, with mid-summer maxima reaching above 100° with some frequency. Clear skies, bright sun, and little wind movement further characterize the summer.

Winter weather is dominated by westerly air flow, which brings recurrent but irregular passage of extratropical cyclones with their associated fronts. Frontal passage usually results in rain, which may be brief and showery or protracted and drizzly. Annual rainfall totals in the region average between 20 and 45 inches, with 20% to 35% of the total falling in the wettest winter month. Winters are not really cold, but there are long stretches of chilly weather, with mid-winter maximum temperatures in the sixties and minima in the forties. Snow is rare, but not unknown.

TASMANIA. The island of Tasmania is far enough south to have a true mid-latitude climate, with warm summers and cold winters. The topographic complexity of the region produces considerable local climatic variations, the most widespread of which involves abundant precipitation on the western slopes and rain shadow conditions in the east. Most of the island receives at least 30 inches of precipitation annually, and some places experience thrice that. Winter is the season of maximum precipitation in the western part of the region; elsewhere a uniform seasonal regime is characteristic. Snow is experienced over most of the island, at least occasionally.

Water Scarce, Water Deep

To the hydrologist and hydrographer Australia is a continent of fascination. The nature, distribution, and amount of surface and sub-surface water has many unusual facets and is comparable, even in its basic aspects, to that of no other continent. In essence, Australia has the smallest supply of surface water and the most remarkable conditions of underground water of any of the settled continents.

HYDROGRAPHY.   The basic fact of Australian hydrography is the scarcity of water. The country lacks the high, young mountain ranges that are found in other parts of the world, so there are no permanent snowfields or glaciers to sustain river flow. Furthermore, orographical precipitation possibilities are limited, to say the least. As a generalization, it can be stated that wherever the annual precipitation is less than about twenty to twenty-five inches, no permanent streamflow can be maintained. Under these conditions, streams are either intermittent (occurring during the wet season or after rains only) or exotic (sustained by waters that enter the drainage system from wetter areas). Thus, nearly three-quarters of the country—all but the northern, eastern, southeastern, and southwestern coasts—is largely without permanent streamflow. Only in the two smallest states, Tasmania and Victoria, do the majority of the principal streams run continuously.

Most of the important Australian rivers have their headwaters in the Eastern Highlands, which serve as the east-west continental drainage divide. In many areas, however, this divide is not at all sharp, and the streams originate in grassy flats or tablelands where the watershed is not clearly defined.

The principal drainage basins are characterized below.

1. The *Carpentaria Basin* is a classic example of a centripetal drainage system, with rivers converging inward toward the Gulf of Carpentaria from distant, slightly elevated uplands to the east, south, and west. Total annual streamflow in the basin is very large, but strictly seasonal. Most of the rivers, with the conspicuous exception of the Gregory and some from the northern Cape York Peninsula, flow only during and immediately after the period of summer monsoon; during the remainder of the year they are mostly dry. The entire drainage basin reflects the importance of monsoonal rainfall. Almost all the rivers cross a very flat coastal plain in their lower courses, and are characterized by much distributary development and mutual discharge into neighboring rivers. Most flow into extensive mangrove swamps on the edge of the Gulf, and many have no outlet to the Gulf proper. The most notable rivers in the Carpentaria Basin are the Roper from the west; the Gregory, Leichhardt, and Flinders from the south; and the Gilbert and Mitchell from the east. This last-mentioned stream may yield the greatest total annual discharge of any river in Australia, even exceeding the Murray, although accurate statistics to verify this claim are not available.
2. The *Mainland Pacific Slope* encompasses a large number of relatively short streams that carry, on balance, a considerable annual flow. Most of the rivers are structurally similar in that they rise fairly near the coast and then flow latitudinally (north or south) in their upper courses for some distance at a gentle gradient before turning more or less abruptly seaward. The monsoonal influence is strong in northern Queensland, and the rivers there have a pronounced flow maxima in summer. Farther south, however, winter is the wetter season, so that most Pacific slope rivers of New South Wales and Victoria carry more water in that season. The greatest annual discharges are from the Tully, Herbert, Burdekin (second only to the Murray in measured annual flow), Fitzroy, Burnett, Richmond, Clarence, Hunter, and Snowy.
3. The drainage systems of *Tasmania* consist of a number of short rivers that

have considerable discharge, due to relatively heavy, year-round precipitation. Many of the streams have broad estuaries at their mouths. Tasmania's largest flow is in the Derwent system, which drains the southeastern part of the island. Other major rivers are the Huon in the south, the South Esk and Mersey in the north, and almost every river on the west coast.

4. The *River Murray system* is by far the most important drainage in Australia, and also the most complex. Total annual discharge from the Murray is about 8 million acre-feet (in comparison to 474 million acre-feet from the Mississippi), but half again that much is withdrawn for irrigation along its course. Except in its high headwaters, the Murray has a remarkably gentle gradient; from Albury to the mouth (more than 1200 miles) the gradient is less than nine inches to the mile, and over more than half that distance it is less than three inches per mile. As might be expected, then, there is considerable development of distributaries and marshes with maze-like channels, although in some areas the stream has a narrow incised valley in a broad floodplain. Major tributaries of the Murray include the Murrumbidgee, which drains the northern slopes of the Snowy Mountains; the Goulburn, from Victoria; and the Darling, a lengthy river with a very erratic flow regime.

5. The drainage systems of *Southwestern Australia* are characterized by a number of relatively short streams that have their upper courses in wide, flattish valleys on the plateau surface and then descend onto the coastal plain and into the sea. Many of the streams empty into lagoons because they are not strong enough to maintain an open entry into the ocean. Their flow regime is often intermittent, with winter as time of maximum discharge.

6. The *Western* drainage systems contain a few long rivers that are almost entirely intermittent in their flow. They have the characteristics of desert streams, normally dry but carrying overflow flood water after the infrequent rains. Evaporation and sinking into the sand take much of the water that would otherwise flow into the Indian Ocean.

7. The *Timor Sea* drainage systems have markedly monsoonal regimes. Extensive floods are common in summer, but during the dry season most of the rivers either dry up completely or are reduced to irregular chains of billabongs (pools or waterholes). The great rivers of this region are the Fitzroy (which drains the southern Kimberleys), the Ord (which drains the eastern Kimberleys), and the Victoria and Daly (in the Northern Territory).

8. The *Lake Eyre Basin* is one of the largest areas of internal drainage in the world. The focus of convergence of this system is a series of interconnected lakes in South Australia, of which Lake Eyre is by far the largest. The lakes are playas, and are normally dry with a heavily salt-encrusted surface of silt and sand. On rare occasions they become water-filled, but never deeply. The principal drainage into the lakes comes from western Queensland via Cooper's Creek and the Diamantina and Georgina rivers. Their waterways make up the famous Channel Country. This region is dry most of the time, but occasionally after a heavy rain an enormous area will be flooded, bringing about a rapid growth of herbage that is much desired for livestock pasturage.

There are other large areas of internal drainage in Australia, as in the Wimmera district of northwestern Victoria or the Bulloo system of south-central Queensland, but the most extensive "drainage" region of all is one that is largely without any sort of surface waterways. This region extends from the Great Sandy Desert in the north to the Amadeus Basin and the Great Victoria Desert in the east to the south edge of the Nullarbor Plain in the south, and occupies about one million acres of land. A few intermittent streams are found, but for the most part this region simply has no surface drainage at all.

UNDERGROUND WATER. In contrast to the scarce surface water, Australia's underground water resources are unusually plentiful. Their quality, unfortunately, does not match their quantity. Actually, the *ground water* supply (water in the saturated zone between the water table and the uppermost impervious layer) is not unusual; indeed, it is distributed about as one might expect in an arid continent. The resources of *confined water* (occupying deeper aquifers under pressure between impervious strata), on the other hand, are quite widespread. The confined water is largely *artesian* (under sufficient pressure to rise to the surface when tapped), though some is *subartesian* (under less pressure, and so will rise only part way to the surface when tapped).

The most famous and by far the most extensive of the underground water supplies is the Great Artesian Basin, which underlies two-thirds of Queensland, much of New South Wales and South Australia, and part of the Northern Territory (Figure 2-2C). This is the largest artesian basin in the world, with several thousand flowing bores (wells) coming from three different aquifers. A number of problems inhibit maximum use of the water, however, particularly depth, temperature, and salinity. In some places the water source is more than 7,000 feet below the surface, significantly increasing the cost of well drilling. Normally the water is quite hot, occasionally with a temperature that rises as much as 1° F. for every ten feet of depth; sometimes the water must be run in an open ditch on the surface for half a mile before it cools sufficiently for cattle to drink it. The dissolved mineral content in the water is usually so high as to make the liquid unsuitable for human use or irrigation purposes, although it is satisfactory for stock watering.

There are other artesian and subartesian basins in Australia, but none nearly as large or as significant as the Great Artesian Basin. In some cases these other basins have better quality water, but for the most part they suffer from the same handicaps as does the Great Artesian Basin.

Subsurface water supplies, then, while vast in extent are poor in quality. They are extremely important to pastoral development, but should not be expected to contribute significantly toward "opening up" the country to farming or urban settlement.

The Skin of the Earth

We have seen that Australia is a land of unusual structure, topography, climate, and hydrography; thus it should come as no surprise that the soil pattern of the country differs in several important aspects from the generalized continental pattern that is found over most of the world.

The appropriate generalization is that the humid soils of Australia are quite similar to their counterparts on other continents, but the Australian arid soils are much less comparable. Presumably, a soil that develops under conditions of considerable leaching will turn out in a "normal" or predictable fashion; that is, the climatic influence will predominate. However, for soils of drier areas the relief or parent material will be a much more significant influence on its development. Thus the ancient, quiescent, and subdued nature of the structure and topography of this continent have left an unusual brand on many of its dry land soils.

As a corollary of this, there is a considerable proportion of ancient and generally impoverished soils in Australia. With a few exceptions, the soils of the continent have a low level of natural fertility, owing to lack of moisture and an inadequate supply of plant nutrients. There is a singular scarcity of phosphorus and nitrogen; only potassium and calcium among the important chemical elements seem to be present in generally adequate quantities. Excess salinity is a major characteristic of many soils and thus a significant land-use problem.

Australian pedologists and agronomists have done a great deal of work on soil problems, particularly on the chemistry of trace elements. The application of their results has meant a notable difference in agricultural and pastoral productivity in many areas; so much so that fertilization is a major factor in Australian consciousness. Such terms as "superphosphate" are now household words (not inappropriately in a country where more than 2,500,000 tons of "super" are applied to the soil annually).

SOIL PATTERNS. Approximately fifty great soil groups have been identified in Australia, and their pattern of distribution is quite complex. In the broadest sense there is a congruency between gross climatic and soil patterns, so that the effect of aridity is clear from any soil distribution map. The reader is reminded, however, that only the most general of soil associations can be shown on a small-scale map like Figure 2-2D; thus, more detailed pedogeographic scrutiny of any part of the continent would demonstrate many variations from the broad pattern.

Humid land soils are restricted largely to east coastal locations, from Cape York to Tasmania, with a small strip along the southwest coast of Western Australia. These are mostly podzolic-type soils that are only partially analogous to types in North America or the Soviet Union. The surface horizons are usually grey, the soils tend to be acidic, and fertility is low to moderate. In a few scattered areas are found red loams called krasnozems that have been developed on basaltic (or similar) bedrock that provides plenty of ferric oxide to keep the soil well flocculated; these are some of the most fertile of Australia's soils.

Subhumid soils are found in a more inland crescent in the east, particularly in New South Wales and southern Queensland, though some also occur in a similar position in Western Australia. A large proportion of the soils in this group consists of blackearths that are similar to typical chernozems, but with a structure that is more likely to be granular or cloddy than crumby and a more limited humus content. Red-brownearths are also widespread in the subhumid zone; they have moderate fertility and can become quite productive with careful management.

Semiarid soils are spread in a ring that goes nearly four-fifths around the heart of the continent. These are quite varied grey and brown soils, often solonized, that are of moderate to low fertility.

Arid land soils include a considerable variety of types and are generally distributed over nearly half the continent. Their color varies, but shades of red and red-brown are predominant. These soils possess a number of unusual characteristics; for example, some of them are distinctly acidic in reaction, in contrast to the alkaline reaction normally expected of desert soils. On the whole the soils of the arid zone can be said to be less fertile than typical desert soils of other continents. Furthermore, there are extensive areas where no true soils have developed, and either gibber plains or largely unanchored sand ridges dominate the surface of the land.

Skeletal soils are widespread in the monsoonal lands of the north, particularly in Western Australia and the Northern Territory. These are poorly developed and thin, and are mostly associated with ranges and tablelands.

A Sclerophyllous World

The natural vegetation of Australia is another environmental facet that exhibits the uniqueness of the land Down Under. Such development is thought to be primarily the result of isolation. It is believed that there have been long periods during the geologic past when the earth's climate was more equable than it is today, with the result that all continents experienced the evolution of relatively similar plant groups. However, since Tertiary time (roughly 3,000,000 years) regional climatic trends have been more disparate, with greater variations and extremes. This has caused the isolation of floras in some parts of the world, engendering specialized evolutionary developments.

The most notable gross feature of the contemporary Australian floristic pattern is the scarcity of dense forest. Nearly all of the continent is vegetated with grassland, shrubland, or relatively open woodland. Furthermore, it is the nature of the dominant tree species (eucalyptus) that their leaf density is relatively sparse and the long narrow leaves hang down inertly, a position that amplifies and emphasizes the openness of the woodland.

Two plant genera are overwhelmingly dominant. The forests, woodlands, and part of the shrublands are largely composed of species of eucalypts (*Eucalyptus* spp.), usually referred to as "gums," whereas much of the rest of the country—shrublands and grasslands—features acacias (*Acacia* spp.), often called "wattles." No other genera are significant enough to be noteworthy. It should be pointed out, of course, that there are hundreds of species of both eucalypts and acacias in Australia.

As is to be expected in an arid continent, much of the Australian flora exhibits pronounced xerophytic (drought-resistant) characteristics, such as deep taproots and great root density to seek moisture in the ground, small and hard leaf surfaces to inhibit transpiration of water, and shiny plant surfaces to reflect rather than absorb solar insolation. Even so, there is a complete absence of native cacti and similar succulent forms that are so common in North American desert areas.

MAJOR VEGETATIONAL ASSOCIATIONS. The broad pattern of natural vegetation in Australia (Figure 2-2E) shows a narrow forest zone (mostly open, sclerophyllous forest, but with scattered patches of dense rain forest) along the east coast and in the extreme southwest. Inland from the forest, and encircling most of the continent, is a zone of woodland, mostly quite open. Farther inland is a complete ring of mixed grassland and shrubland. In the core of the continent, but displaced toward the west, is an extensive area dominated by true desert, where mineral matter is much more dominant than the relatively sparse vegetation.

Rain forest occurs in small, discontinuous patches scattered along the entire east coast, from Cape York to southern New South Wales, although the principal concentrations are in Queensland. This is essentially tropical rain forest, which grows only in response to abundant precipitation, typically at least sixty inches annually, and protection from the drying effect of day-long sun; hence, occurrences are limited mostly to north- and east-facing slopes. It is an evergreen forest comprised of a great variety of species, which are mostly Malaysian in origin (and in which eucalyptus is almost entirely absent). There is normally a dense, interlacing canopy, beneath which there may be one or two other layers acting as discontinuous subcanopies. Lianas and epiphytes are characteristically interspersed. A large area of temperate rain forest, characterized by smaller trees and a lack of parasitic growth, occurs in northwestern Tasmania, and there are smaller patches in Victoria.

Much more extensive is the *sclerophyll forest* association, which is the dominant vegetation within 100 miles of the coast of New South Wales and most of Victoria, and also occupies much of Tasmania and the southwestern corner of Western Australia. This is an essentially eucalyptus forest community made up of medium to tall trees with crowns that form a relatively complete and interlacing canopy. Undergrowth may be dense, but is usually relatively open.

More extensive still is the *woodland* association, comprised of an open, tree-dominated community. This is the principal plant association of the north, of most of the eastern third of Queensland, and of a large area inland from the forest zone of New South Wales, Victoria, and Western Australia. The trees are of varying height and their branches do not interlace into a canopy; thus, there is a distinctly open aspect to the growth. There may or may not be undergrowth, but a grassy understory is typical.

The Australian *shrublands* generally occupy the southern half of the continent except where there is forest, woodland, or desert. The term "shrubland" refers to a considerable variety of shrubform associations that may grow either densely or openly, may or may not be considerably intermingled with grasses, and may be extensive or discontinuous in pattern. In some cases the dominant species take a tree form, but they are never very tall. A special shrubland association is the *mallee*, a name applied to country in which any of a number of distinctively shaped eucalypts grow; they are low trees or tall shrubs with many stems branching from a subsurface rootstock (lignotuber). Also notable are the extensive shrubby steppelands dominated by a bluebush-saltbush (*Kochia* spp.-*Atriplex* spp.) association, which look much like the sagebrush plains of the western United States but are valuable for livestock browsing.

Grassland associations cover much of the northern and eastern interior of the country. The grasses are often interspersed with scattered trees or varied shrubs, particularly near the moister margins. Most of the grassland areas are covered with discrete tussocks rather than a continuous sod; thus "tussock grassland" is a proper term of widespread application. Extensive grasslands of special interest include the Mitchell grass downs (excellent grazing lands dominated by *Astrebla* spp.) and spinifex associations (where great spiky clumps of *Triodia* spp. dominate).

Much of the interior of the country, extending well into the northwest, is true *desert*, and hence very sparsely vegetated. A scattering of xerophytic grasses (mostly annuals) and shrubs is found, and low trees sometimes grow in the dry watercourses.

MAN'S INFLUENCE ON THE FLORA.   The preceding discussion refers to natural vegetation, much of which has been severely modified by human activities and influences. In many areas the original flora has completely disappeared, as a result of clearing the land for farming or some other intensive use, or from pastoral activities.

The principal form of land use in Australia is pastoralism, and most stockmen are eager to improve their grazing conditions by any means. "Improvement" of the land often involves the elimination of trees to make more room for grasses; this is frequently accomplished by "ringbarking," or girdling the tree. Exotic grasses are sometimes introduced to upgrade the pasturage, so that vast acreages of Australia are now sown to such things as crested wheat grass from the Soviet Union and bluegrass from the United States.

A few other significant exotic plants have been introduced into Australia. During the 1920's prickly-pear cactus (*Opuntia* sp.) was brought into Queensland and northern New South Wales, and quickly infested more than 50,000,000 acres before it was essentially eliminated. Much more satisfying has been the introduction of various species of coniferous trees in an effort to establish a softwood lumber industry. Every state now has prospering plantations of exotic pines, primarily *Pinus radiata* from California.

A Faunal Asylum

Of all the Australian environmental elements, none is so remarkable as its fauna; its assemblage of terrestrial animal life is completely without parallel in other parts of the world, and even its bird life is significantly different from that of other continents. The literature of zoogeography abounds with hypotheses as to how this came about. For our purposes here we need only note that the Austral continent functioned as a sort of dead end of evolution, cut off from effective contact with most of the rest of the world's land biota for millions of years, and this fortuity nurtured the flourishing of rare and vulnerable species. Thus, the terrestrial fauna of Australia is bizarre in the extreme. Placental mammals, the dominant animals of other continents, are limited and inconspicuous in Australia. Although more than 100 placental species are recognized, they are all bats, rats, or mice. The "normal" placental groups—ungulates, primates, felines, canids, mustellids, and others—are totally absent.

The characteristic mammals of Australia are marsupials, relatively primitive types that give birth to partially developed, almost embryonic young, which develop after birth for a long period in the mother's pouch. The dominance of marsupials over a long period of time is reflected by the variety of species that has developed and the diversity of ecological niches that these species have filled. In the course of their persistent radiation, they have converged to a remarkable degree, ranging from treetop herbivores to nocturnal predators.

The Australian marsupials include a dozen Recent families, embodying more than 150 living species. The majority are herbivorous types, including the well-known macropods (kangaroos and wallabies), of which there are about four dozen species; the numerous rat kangaroos; the bulky wombats, which are badger-like diggers; tree-dwelling phalangers and possums, numbering some forty species; and the single species of koala. There are also a number of carnivorous marsupials, mostly small, including thirty species of marsupial "mice," a number of marsupial "moles," various "cats" and "devils," the almost-extinct Tasmanian "wolf," and a group of numbats (anteaters). Finally, there are about twenty species of omnivorous marsupials, called bandicoots. These various marsupials range widely over Australia, but are found nowhere else in the world except New Guinea and some associated islands.

As an acme of primitive Mammalia, Australia is also the home of the world's only contemporary monotremes, the duck-bill platypus (*Ornithorhynchus anatinus*) and the spiny anteater (*Tachyglossus aculeatus*). These are the only egg-laying mammals to be found anywhere.

Australia also has a numerous and varied reptilian fauna. Although turtles and tortoises are limited, there are some 240 species of lizards, including some large ones. Two species of crocodile inhabit the northern rivers and lagoons. Snakes are numerous both in quantity and variety.

Bird life is exceedingly varied, with more than 650 species recorded. Especially notable are the psittacine (parrot-like) types, which occur in greater diversity than on any other continent. Two of the world's largest land birds, the emu and the cassowary, are also notable.

Lesser forms of animal life are more limited. Amphibians, for example, are conspicuously few, represented by only a few frogs and toads. Fresh water fishes are also restricted by the general paucity of surface waters. Insects and associated arthropods, on the other hand, are quite abundant;

particularly notable are flies, white ants (termites), ants, butterflies, and mosquitoes.

In addition to native forms of wildlife, a conspicuous element in the present faunal complement of Australia is comprised of foreign species that have been introduced to the continent, by accident or design, and have become established in the wild. Earliest of these exotic introductions was the dingo (*Canis familiaris dingo*), which apparently was brought to Australia by early aboriginal migrants from Southeast Asia, and has been a well-established member of the fauna for many centuries. The most notable recent introduction was that of the European rabbit (*Oryctolagus cuniculus*), whose spread from an initial introduction of twenty-four animals near Melbourne in 1859 to a half-continent plague within fifty years is the classic scare story of all mammalian importations. The diffusion of the European fox (*Vulpes vulpes*) over Australia was even more expansive, and a number of other exotic forms of wildlife have been introduced in lesser proportions. Furthermore, many varieties of livestock have reverted to a feral existence: most numerous are feral pigs, horses, donkeys, camels, and water buffalo, but populations of feral cattle, goats, dogs, and cats are also present.

The First Australians

The unique Australian environment that has been sketched in this chapter provided a home for a distinctive society of primitive people referred to simply as Australian Aborigines. This society, with its Paleolithic culture, was well adjusted to the harsh realities of life on an arid continent and existed for many centuries before the coming of Europeans to the Antipodes.

Their genesis is indistinct, but it is thought that they originated many thousands of years ago in the general area of the East Indies, whence they migrated to Asia (where remnants are still found in Malaya and India), to New Guinea (where further remnants exist), and to Australia. It is believed that they were least changed by amalgamation with other peoples in Australia, and so have maintained their racial characteristics substantially unaltered there.

They are usually classified as Australoid people, not fitting into the three commonly recognized racial categories. Although there were many variations in appearance, a general description might note the following: medium height; wavy but not wooly hair; brown or yellow-brown skin color; retreating forehead but massive eyebrow ridge; much hair on face and body; slim build in males (females are less slim); and remarkably slender legs in both sexes.

They led a wandering existence, and had no permanent homes, often living for months at a time without any sort of constructed shelter. In some cases, particularly in the wetter areas, they might construct temporary "wurlies" or "humpies" or lean-to shelters. Their nomadic movements were not patternless, for each group was restricted by mutual agreement to a broadly defined territory beyond which they strayed only under unusual circumstances. It is thought that there were some 500 tribes, and each tribe recognized the territoriality of others. Within each tribe there were usually several "hordes" of a few dozen people each, and normally every horde had as its nucleus a small "clan" or descent-group.

They did not know agriculture and had no domesticated plants or animals, except the dog, which is presumably the source of the dingo. Thus, their livelihood depended entirely upon hunting and gathering. The normal division of labor called for men to hunt and women to gather; successful hunting meant good eating, but day-to-day subsistence was more directly dependent upon the success of the women as they gathered and dug roots, berries, grubs, lizards, and other Outback delicacies. Their way of life was a continuous round of hunting and gathering, interrupted with some frequency for ceremonies. The bushcraft of the aborigines (both male and female) has been a subject of awe. They were, and are, remarkably adept as practical naturalists and as trackers.

They had few material possessions, apparently not wanting to be encumbered in their nomadic wanderings. Captain James Cook, perhaps the first European to have significant contact with aborigines, remarked in wonder at their lack of interest in the gifts he gave them, a reaction that was in distinct contrast to his experience with any other native group.

They covet not magnificent houses, household stuff, etc.; they live in a warm and fine climate, and enjoy every wholesome air, so that they have very little need of clothing; and this they seem to be fully sensible of, for many to whom we gave cloth, etc., left it carelessly upon the sea beach and in the woods, as a thing they had no manner of use for; in short, they seemed to set no value upon anything we gave them, nor would they ever part with anything of their own for any one article we could offer them. This, in my opinion, argues that they think themselves provided with all the necessaries of life, and that they have no superfluities.[1]

Characteristically, the Aborigines wore no clothing, except perhaps a skin cloak in wetter and colder areas. Their weapons and tools varied from group to group (the boomerang, for example, might be an important weapon for some, a musical instrument for others, and unknown to others), but were invariably limited in number and variety. Typical items might include spears, woomera (spear-thrower), stone axe, net, and digging stick. Often these objects would be intricately designed with art forms of religious or magical significance. Household utensils were also few; most common would be a water bag and dilly bag (for carrying food), both made of skins.

What the Aborigines lacked in material possessions (and their material culture surely ranked among the simplest in the world), they made up for in nonmaterial aspects. They had an extraordinarily complex set of religious and magical beliefs, superstitions, and taboos, based largely

---

[1] Christopher Lloyd, ed., *The Voyages of Captain James Cook Round the World* (London: The Cresset Press, 1949), p. 87.

upon an elaborate oral mythology that emphasized the "dreamtime," a vague past in which animistic spirits worked creative wonders on the earth. The artistic expression of their spiritual beliefs involved cave paintings, wood carvings, unique bark paintings, rhythmic dances, and intricate charade-games and rituals.

The total population of Aborigines in Australia at the time of European contact is estimated to be in the neighborhood of 300,000. Their scattered occupancy encompassed the entire continent, including Tasmania. However, there was no cohesiveness of development, no large political or social organization, and for the most part there was little contact between different tribes or groups except those adjacent to one another. Linguistic variety was great, with dozens of mutually unintelligible dialects and languages spoken in different areas.

To summarize, the Australian Aborigines were relatively few, racially apart from the rest of the world, naked hunters and gatherers, houseless, artistic in a primitive way, mystical, and enclosed within firm and intricate social patterns. Thus, they were essentially Stone Age people fitted to survive in a fierce and generally unproductive habitat as long as there was no significant competition with more advanced peoples.

CHAPTER 3 *peopling*
the austral continent

The history of Australia is quiet and relatively uneventful. If one's concept of history is focussed on the dramatic, then Australia has no history. There were no invasions, no civil wars, no revolutions, not even any formidable opposition from indigenes. Australia is a nation that grew in relatively tame and orderly fashion from its first convict settlement to federation in little more than a century.

The ancient and remote Austral continent provided a secluded home for bizarre biota and primitive natives for dozens of centuries. This pristine land was undoubtedly touched by East Indian sailors or Malayan fishermen from time to time, but their imprint was almost nil. Despite speculation and prediction of the presence of a southern continent, European attention to the Southwest Pacific was slow in materializing; it was not until the seventeenth century that European navigators coasted Australian waters.

Legends and rumors concerning the existence of an Austral (southern) land mass had been prevalent sporadically since the second century A.D. (Ptolemy's time). Ancient literature was replete with references to a mysterious southern continent called Terra Australis, although its location and dimensions were vague.

Discovery

It is not known who was the first foreigner to set eyes on Australia, to "discover" the continent from the European point of view. As with various other parts of the Pacific, there is some speculation that Spanish and Portuguese navigators may have viewed sections of the Australian coastline before 1600, but no actual records of such occurrences have been found. Earliest evidence dates from 1606, when Luis Vaez de Torres sailed between Queensland and New Guinea in the strait that now bears his name, but even this contact was inadequately recorded, and the Torres Strait did not appear on maps until more than one and a half centuries later.

In that same year a Dutch sea captain named Willem Jansz sailed down the west coast of Cape York Peninsula for some distance, and he is given credit by some authorities for discovering Australia. His opinion of the land was contemptuous ("no good to be done there") and did little to encourage future developments. During the succeeding three decades at least nine other Dutch vessels explored the Australian coast, most of them inadvertently, having been blown too far west when sailing with the prevailing westerlies from South Africa to Java. In this fashion the coastline came to be known and recorded incompletely, from the Great Bight around the western and northern sides to Cape York. The Dutch captains, however, were interested primarily in the East Indies, and they were generally unimpressed with the arid and semiarid coasts that they found. Still, they charted most of the west coast, and it appeared on Dutch maps by 1620.

Abel Tasman was the last of the Dutch sailors associated with the history of "New Holland," as Australia was then called. In the early 1640's his broad circumnavigation of the continent (he went around New Zealand and New Guinea at the same time) offered the first definite proof that it was not connected with any other major land mass. On the same voyage he discovered Tasmania, which he named Van Diemen's Land after the Dutch Governor of Java.

William Dampier was the first Englishman known to visit Australia. He explored along the northwest coast in 1688 and again in 1699. He experienced miserable weather and came away with little favorable to report to the Admiralty, discouraging further exploration for many years. Apart from these two contacts by Dampier, it was well over a century after Tasman's voyages before there was any other exploration of significance in Australian waters.

Captain James Cook, the greatest of the Pacific explorers, contributed significantly to the European settlement of Australia. He was anxious to prove the existence (or lack of same) of a great southern continent and its relationship with New Holland and New Zealand. In 1770, on the first of his three major voyages, he spent some five months along the east coast of Australia. He was the first European to spend much time on the humid margin of the continent and transmitted favorable reports to England. Cook claimed the land for George III, named it New South Wales, and charted much of the eastern coastline.

Initial Settlements

As a more or less direct result of Cook's evaluation, the colonization of Australia from Britain was begun. The First Fleet consisted of an eleven-ship prison convoy, which carried some 800 convicts, 200 marine guards, and 400 other persons to a landing at Botany Bay in January,

1788. Governor Arthur Phillip soon recognized the limitations of the area for settlement, and transferred the entire colony to the next bay northward (Port Jackson Bay), where the Sydney settlement was founded and where the city of Sydney stands today (see Figure 3-1). This was the principal nucleus for the colonization of the continent.

The second settlement was established in the estuary of the Derwent River in Van Diemen's Land. Two groups of settlers, many of them convicts, were landed in 1803 and 1804, and Hobart Town was founded. This Tasmanian colony was designed as a convict settlement, but it was also proposed to test the possibilities of grain cultivation, timber export, and sealing. The final stimulus for settlement was fear that the French might try to settle there first.

Another colony was started in Van Diemen's Land in 1804, this time on the north coast. Some 180 persons, about half of them convicts, were landed. The settlement was shifted twice, but became stabilized in 1806 on the present site of Launceston. Other settlers soon came to the island, from the mainland of New South Wales, from Norfolk Island (where another convict colony had been established), and from Britain. By 1810 the population of Van Diemen's Land numbered more than 1,300, including about 250 convicts.

The second settlement on the mainland was originally more or less an "out-station" from Sydney. After a couple of false starts, a small number of convicts was shifted to Newcastle, at the mouth of the Hunter River about 100 miles north of Sydney. An abundance of nearby bituminous coal helped to assure the success of the settlement, even though it was primarily a penal station for a number of years.

Several attempts were made to settle in what is now Victoria (it was called the Port Phillip District of New South Wales until separation in 1851), from as early as 1803. The first involved more than 400 people, but the colony was abandoned within four months and the settlers moved on to Hobart. Several other abortive settlements were made before the first "permanent" squatters (settlers without legal land grants or even governmental permission) arrived in the early 1830's. Many more squatters, often from Van Diemen's Land, arrived in the mid-thirties; in 1836, at which time the district had some 200 European inhabitants, an official government settlement was proclaimed. The settlement nucleus, originally called Bearbrass, was renamed Melbourne in 1837 and grew more rapidly than any of the other original Australian settlement centers.

The first settlement in what is now Queensland dates from 1824, when thirty convicts and their guards were landed at Redcliffe, on the southeastern coast. Later that year Governor Brisbane (of New South Wales) ordered the removal of the colony, which was subsequently named after him, to a more propitious location a few miles inland. By 1830 the Brisbane colony contained about 1,000 convicts and 100 soldiers. The first free settlers began to "squat" in the Darling Downs (inland from Brisbane) in 1838; four years later the prison colony was abandoned and the area was officially thrown open to free settlement.

Several settlements were attempted on the north central coast of Aus-

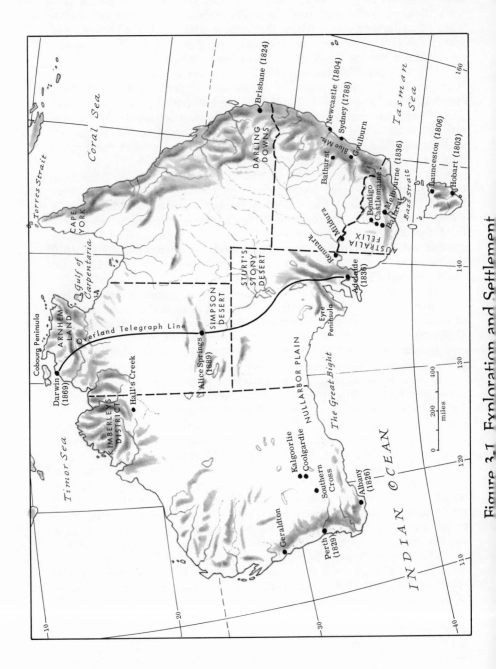

Figure 3-1 Exploration and Settlement

tralia, in the general vicinity of the present location of Darwin, in the 1820's and 1830's. Harsh conditions, remote location, and human foibles resulted in their all being abandoned before the midpoint of the nineteenth century.

In order to enhance Britain's claim to the entire continent and to forestall anticipated French settlement, a group of settlers was landed at Frederickstown (the present-day Albany), in what is now Western Australia, in 1826. A more permanent settlement was established on the Swan River, where Perth is now located, three years later. The colony did not prosper, however. There were notable plans for free settlement, but a combination of ignorance, lack of manpower, and minimal government support diluted the effort. The population had reached 4,000 in 1830, but dwindled to less than 1,000 by 1832.

The last of the initial settlements was in many ways the most interesting and innovative. South Australia was founded in 1836 as a planned colony based on free enterprise and an orderly design for settlement. It was unique among the initial colonies in that convicts were never involved. Settlement was organized by a land settlement company, conceived by British social theoreticians (especially Edward Gibbon Wakefield), and backed by British capitalists. The harsh realities of the new land presented many difficulties, but the colony struggled forward until 1842, when an administrative reorganization centralized more authority under the Crown. The colony registered continued, if erratic, growth in its early years.

Exploration by Sea and by Land

The coasts of Australia, understandably, were well known long before the early settlers had any real concept of the inland. Most of the coastline was charted, at least in a generalized fashion, before the end of the eighteenth century. The south coast was the last to be surveyed. George Bass and Matthew Flinders sailed through Bass Strait for the first time in 1798, and proved that Van Diemen's Land was an island. Flinders surveyed most of the rest of the south coast in 1800–1802. The French navigator, Baudin, also charted much of that coast in 1802. Ironically, the very last part of the Australian coast to be surveyed was around the mouth of the continent's only large river (the Murray), at Encounter Bay (where Flinders and Baudin met).

Exploration by land was incidental to settlement and began only after the Sydney penal colony was thoroughly established. Mostly the overland exploration was practical in intent and empirical in method. The initial goal was to find good farming land, and later it was to discover good pastoral land. When explorers were successful in these endeavors, settlers were rarely far behind.

Overland exploration was beset by numerous difficulties. The most immediate problem was to break out of the relatively small lowland that encircled Port Jackson Bay on the three landward sides. Rugged, sterile sandstone ranges cut the Sydney colony off from the interior.

The tumbled gorges and scarps of the Blue Mountains presented precipitous slopes that defied penetration for more than a quarter of a century after initial settlement. And although the mountains were finally crossed for the first time in 1813, they remained a formidable obstacle to effective penetration of the interior for some time to come.

Once these mountains were breached, the true nature of the Australian continent began to assert itself. Further penetration was slow because of a scarcity of that most precious of commodities—water. Living off the land was often difficult because food resources were inadequate. Other problems included high temperatures, persistently bothersome insects, and sometimes, Aboriginal hostility.

The first of the major inland explorers was Charles Sturt, who spent the better part of two decades (the 1820's and 1830's) investigating the interior of New South Wales. His expeditions contributed immensely to an understanding of the complex river pattern and regime in that region. He finally succeeded in tracing the River Murray to its mouth, perhaps the most important single exploration in Australian history.

At about this same time there were various less ambitious explorations from the Sydney colony southward into the Port Phillip District, westward to the plains of Goulburn and Bathurst, and northward toward Queensland. Reports from these expeditions stimulated the movement of settlers in all three directions; although initial response often was only a trickle of migrants, these streams became floods before long.

Most settlement stayed fairly close to the east coast then, but explorers became more daring, and began to make deeper penetrations into the Outback. There was a continuing interest in the inland. Although from the fringe it looked remarkably like a semi-desert, hope sprung eternally that it would prove to contain fertile farm or grazing land. Many people grappled with personal obsessions that exploration of the interior would reveal an inland sea, or an inland river system, or a high mountain range serving as a watershed divide. All of these hopes were forlorn, of course, but they nourished fruitful results, for they stimulated the exploration of the continent.

The first major exploration northward was that of Ludwig Leichhardt, a German scientist of mystical bent, who traversed from the Darling Downs of southeastern Queensland to the Cobourg Peninsula of Arnhem Land in 1844–45. His route was paralleled in part by an 1845–46 expedition led by Major Thomas Mitchell, which succeeded in exploring a large part of interior Queensland. This was only one of a number of significant explorations by Mitchell, who had previously surveyed much of the interior of New South Wales and had penetrated into the fertile western portion of Victoria, which he called Australia Felix.

The first east-west crossing of the continent was accomplished by E. J. Eyre in the early 1840's. He was the leader of a South Australian government expedition that had been intended to seek a feasible livestock route to the west coast from Adelaide. At Eyre's insistence, the purpose of the expedition was changed to a search for the center of the continent. However, unusual rains bogged the party at Lake Torrens, so they had to go westward after all. Eyre finally succeeded in crossing the Nullarbor Plain, accompanied by a single Aborigine, and he reached Albany after one of the classic journeys in the history of exploration. Unfortunately, this remarkable walk resulted in little information of practical value, as the participants were forced to follow the coastline most of the way.

Charles Sturt had shifted his interest from New South Wales to South Australia by the 1840's. His last expedition, an heroic failure to reach the center of Australia, covered eighteen months in 1844–46. He was stopped by drought conditions and turned back by the gibbered surface of Sturt's Stony Desert and the sand ridges of the Simpson Desert.

Ludwig Leichhardt's final imprint on the Australian continent was a question mark. In 1848 he led an expedition westward from Brisbane, in an attempt to cross to the west coast. With six companions and nearly 300 head of livestock, he disappeared and was never heard from again. No definite traces of the expedition were ever found, and its actual fate is the great mystery of Australian exploration history.

The first successful south-north crossing of the continent was accomplished by the famous Burke and Wills expedition in 1860–61. After starting from Melbourne with an unwieldy expedition of twenty men, twenty-six camels, and twenty-three horses, they slimmed down to a smaller party (four men, six camels, and one horse) at Cooper's Creek and made a "dash" to the north coast. Favored by good weather, they reached the Gulf of Carpentaria without major difficulty, but the return journey was an almost complete tragedy. The horse, four of the camels, and three of the men perished. Furthermore, their surveying had been inadequate and the leader (Robert Burke) had not even kept a journal.

Simultaneously, an expedition led by John McDouall Stuart was working its way northward from Adelaide. This was Stuart's sixth penetration of the interior (he had reached the center of the continent on his fourth journey, in 1860), and he successfully reached the north coast in 1862. His careful survey and favorable report led directly to settlement in the Northern Territory and to the construction of the Overland Telegraph Line, completed in 1872, from Adelaide to Darwin. This line, in a sense, separated the semi-explored eastern half of the continent from the totally unexplored western half. To that date only Eyre had crossed Australia from east to west, and he had been in sight of the southern coastline essentially all the way.

Colonel P. E. Warburton led a significant east-west crossing in 1873–74. His expedition traveled from Adelaide to Alice Springs and thence westward. Warburton had planned to reach the central coast of Western Australia, but dry conditions kept forcing the party northwestward. It was a fearful journey, and although none of the seven men perished, all just barely survived. This was the first Australian exploring expedition to use camels as the sole means of transport, and it is generally agreed that the hardy nature of these beasts was the only factor that prevented the expedition from ending in total tragedy.

John Forrest, a young and vigorous Western Australian, reversed the normal route and led two expeditions from west to east in the early

1870's. He traveled from Perth to Adelaide in 1872 and from Geraldton to the Overland Telegraph Line two years later. Forrest was later appointed the first premier of the colony, and after federation he served in the federal parliament for eighteen years.

Ernest Giles, a man of great drive, led five separate expeditions in South Australia and Western Australia in the 1870's, including a double crossing of the continent (east-west and west-east). His explorations led to a filling in of the last major blanks on the map of Australia, and he is therefore generally regarded as the last of the major Australian explorers. Thus ended the heroic era.

The Early Spread of Settlement

The settlement at Sydney was established as a penal colony, but almost immediately it began to be something more. The convicts were not able to make themselves self-sufficient, a fact which hastened the rather stormy transition from jail to free colony. Agricultural production was the greatest need, and there were many attempts at farming. However, for the first thirty years or so the settlement was restricted to a small area around the original nucleus, which contained an inadequate amount of good farmland. There were limited tracts of shale and silt that harbored soils that would support crops, but the settlement was essentially hemmed in by a vast belt of unproductive sandstones and abrupt slopes. Thus foodstuffs and other essential supplies had to be brought from the other side of the world for several decades, a necessity which made life in the new land precarious.

Very early it became clear that the area would never be fruitful for farming, so emphasis turned to stock raising. Several varieties of livestock were imported, but the Merino sheep turned out to be far and away the most suitable. The emphasis on breeding and raising sheep for wool production, particularly fostered by John MacArthur in the early years of the nineteenth century, changed the entire course of development of the colony and sheep raising became the economic lifeblood of the continent for many decades to come.

As sheep raising developed, there was much desire to push beyond the narrow confines of the Sydney area. Official governmental policy was against this tendency, because of difficulties of managing and policing away from the centralized settlement. However, during the second decade of the nineteenth century, explorers were finally able to open routes across the barrier of the Blue Mountains. Settlement quickly spread to the Bathurst Plains on the west and to the Goulburn Plains on the southwest, and within a few years the frontier of expansion was advancing outward in all directions from Sydney. By the 1830's there were more free settlers than convicts in Australia (see Figure 3-2), and by 1840 pastoralists were ensconced as far south as Australia Felix, as far west as Spencer Gulf, and as far north as the Darling Downs. Thus the central section of New South Wales, as the entire eastern part of Australia was then called, experienced much settlement expansion during the 1830's and 1840's.

All of the humid and subhumid portions of the region were occupied, and even the semiarid plains of the west received a share of the expanding population. Some of this activity involved large land settlement companies from Britain, but most was of the individual settler and squatter type. Presaging even greater mining activity in all the Australian colonies a few years later, coal mining got an early start in the Hunter Valley. The first boatload of coal was shipped to Sydney in 1801, and by 1814 there was a thriving coal trade with India. The Hunter Valley was very attractive to agricultural settlers from the 1820's onward.

Van Diemen's Land, although primarily a penal colony, was producing both sheep and wheat at an early stage. Settlement spread up the Derwent and Macquarie valleys and along the north coast. Whaling and sealing thrived at various coastal towns, and wheat was being exported to the mainland by 1820. Agitation for separation from New South Wales grew, and Van Diemen's Land (the name was not changed to Tasmania for another thirty years) became a separate colony in 1825, at which time there were some 15,000 Europeans on the island, nearly half of them still convicts. Fights between settlers and Aborigines reached a peak about this time, and there were other civil problems; but population, livestock numbers, and crop production continued to expand with considerable rapidity.

Although a few squatters had come to the Port Phillip District early, the population was still very sparse around Melbourne until the latter part of the 1830's. The number of Europeans in the district increased from about 200 in 1836 to nearly 10,000 in 1840; sheep numbers in this same period grew from 25,000 to 800,000. Mitchell's favorable report on Australia Felix was a major stimulus to settlement expansion. Here, as always, exploration was largely at the behest of potential settlers, who followed close on the heels of the explorers. The tide of squatters and other settlers spread rapidly in the central and western parts of the district, and most of the usable pastoral land was occupied by 1845. In 1851, when Victoria became a separate colony, it contained an estimated 77,000 settlers and 5,000,000 sheep.

From the time the Moreton Bay area was opened to freemen in the early 1840's, the settlement history of Queensland was one of cattle expansion to the north, northwest, and west. Overlanders and their herds followed such explorers as Leichhardt and Mitchell, Kennedy and Gregory, and took up large pastoral holdings with or without proper title to the land. A scarcity of labor and inadequate contact with Sydney led to agitation for separation from New South Wales. Queensland became a separate colony in 1859, with a European population of about 25,000.

In South Australia, as we have seen, the first years were difficult ones. Settlement expansion was carefully controlled so that there was orderly growth rather than "leapfrogging" outward from Adelaide. However, economic improvement was slow until the mid-1840's, when sheep, wheat, and copper contributed to prosperity and to settlement expansion eastward and southward, but particularly northward. Between 1840 and 1850 the population of the colony increased from 14,000 to 63,000, the

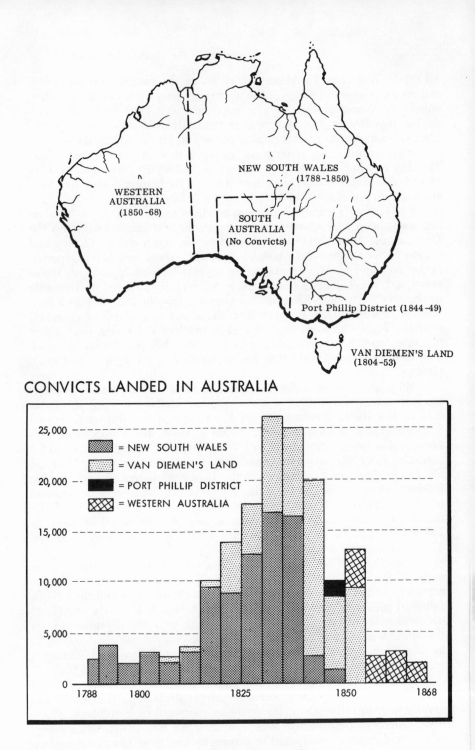

CONVICTS LANDED IN AUSTRALIA

Figure 3-2 Convicts in Early Australia

CONVICTS AND FREE MIGRANTS

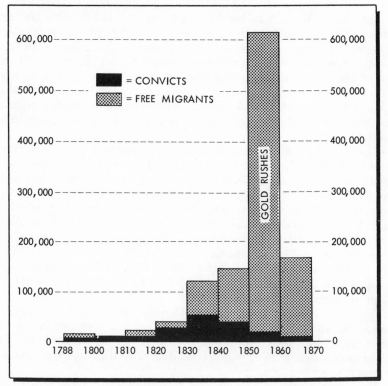

Adapted from Ian Wynd and Joyce Wood, *A Map History of Australia,* 2nd edition. (Melbourne: Oxford University Press, 1967), p. 11. By permission of the publisher.

number of sheep from 200,000 to 1,000,000, and the wheat acreage from 1,000 to 41,000.

The colony of Western Australia experienced the most desultory growth pattern of all. Unproductive soil and dense stands of timber inhibited much settlement expansion, and the colony all but stagnated during the 1830's and 1840's. Eventually convicts were brought in in order to provide cheap labor for economic stimulation, so Western Australia became a penal colony between 1850 and 1868; still, settlement expansion was limited until the gold rush days later in the century.

Eastern Gold Rushes

Although Australia's settlement history was relatively peaceful, it was not without excitement, and the most exciting and dynamic times were associated with the discovery and exploitation of gold deposits.

Each of the major gold rushes followed a similar pattern—hopeful men stampeded to the diggings from near and far, coming from all over Australia, from California, from Britain, and from China. The population expanded spectacularly for a few years, and then the counterflow began. Most of the miners either drifted away or settled down into more mundane occupations such as farmer, pastoralist, or storekeeper. The aftermath of a gold rush, then, invariably contributed significantly to settlement expansion, to increased agricultural and pastoral production, and to urban growth.

The first and greatest sequence of gold rushes took place in Victoria, beginning in 1851. There were numerous strikes, but the major ones were at Ballarat, Bendigo, and Castlemaine. The gold was mostly in alluvial deposits, so miners needed only simple equipment. Literally hundreds of thousands of people were attracted to the colony—from Tasmania, from South Australia, and from all over the world—including some 20,000 Chinese, whose arrival led to Oriental exclusion immigration restrictions. The population of Victoria increased from 70,000 to half a million in less than eight years. The peak of gold production was achieved in 1856, but the population influx gave a matchless impetus to the agricultural and industrial sectors of the economy.

New South Wales experienced gold rushes at the same time as Victoria, in the early 1850's. The strikes were smaller, more scattered, and shorter lived, with peak production dating from 1852. Nevertheless, significant population growth was recorded, and settlement expansion was considerably accelerated.

Gold was discovered in each of the other eastern colonies during this same decade, but the yields were small and the rushes were insignificant in comparison to those of Victoria and New South Wales.

Filling in the Pattern

In New South Wales, Victoria, and Tasmania, and to a lesser extent in the three other colonies, the middle of the nineteenth century was a time of considerable unrest and disorder, analogous in many ways to the "Wild West" period of American history. Land ownership patterns were at the root of the problem. There had been large grants of land, and many of these holdings had been further pyramided. Other settlers often "squatted" on the land illegally, and the entire matter of land alienation and ownership was strife-laden. There was much agitation for small land grants to be made to landless individuals, so' that they could make a start as farmers or pastoralists.

This general situation led to a certain amount of land reform, and it also resulted in the "bushranger" era of Australian history. Bushrangers were essentially outlaws or highwaymen who robbed banks, towns, and especially coaches. Although part of the rural scene in the eastern colonies from the earliest days of settlement (the first bushrangers were escaped convicts), it wasn't until the 1860's that bushranging reached its heyday of activity. Many bushrangers of that period (such as Ned Kelly, Ben Hall, and Captain Moonlight) have become leading Australian folk heroes.

During the latter half of the twentieth century the settlement of Queensland was diffused and intensified by several factors. Cattlemen continued to settle all over the colony, pushing the frontier outward and filling in many of the gaps. Furthermore, sheep were brought into the central plains in increasing numbers, and the foundations for the present distribution pattern (sheep in the center and south; cattle in the west, north, and east) were established. Specialized tropical agriculture got its start around Brisbane in 1862 with the first sugar cane plantation. Despite a shortage of local labor, cane production spread northward to occupy most of the fertile coastal valleys between the New South Wales border and Cape York Peninsula. Natives of various Pacific islands, called "kanakas," were imported to work on the sugar plantations, causing considerable uproar among the labor-conscious European population. After a quarter of a century kanakas were prohibited from entry, but nearly 50,000 of them had been brought in by that time. Despite Queensland's vast extent, most of the colony except for Cape York was occupied by settlers by the 1880's.

The spread of settlement in South Australia became less orderly with the passage of time. The Eyre Peninsula attracted sheepmen and farmers; cattle raising became important in the cooler, more humid areas of the southeast; the lower Murray basin attracted settlers and entrepreneurs, partly for farming and partly to participate in river commerce; and sheep-wheat farmers spread northward into the Flinders Ranges. At its greatest extent, wheat was being grown as far as Wilpena Pound, but the unusually ample rainfall that had attracted farmers that far north soon gave way to more usual conditions, resulting in a rollback of the farming frontier to the south of Goyder's Line (a line marking the northward margin of country deemed by the colony's Surveyor-General to be capable of growing wheat in normal years). A significant drain on the colony's budget during these years was the administration of the Northern Territory, which was governed by South Australia from 1862 till 1911.

Successful settlement was tardy in the Northern Territory. Even the completion of the Overland Telegraph Line did not serve as much of a stimulus. The town of Palmerston (later renamed Darwin) was begun in 1869, and Stuart (later to become Alice Springs) was not laid out until two decades later. There were various gold discoveries in the 1860's and 1870's, but they were not nearly as notable as the strikes in the eastern colonies. The gold did attract Chinese, however, and there was a considerable influx of Orientals in the last quarter of the nineteenth century. Pastoralists did not pay much attention to the Northern Territory until the 1880's, when herds of cattle began to be overlanded from Queensland. In a relatively short time much of the northern part of the territory (the "Top End") was divided into pastoral properties, and some pastoralists were established in the Alice Springs district (the "Centre") as well. The territory's first railway was a 100-mile line built from Palmerston to Pine Creek in 1889.

Gold was the most important stimulus to settlement in Western Australia. Although Perth had been connected to Albany by a 250-mile road through the impressive Jarrah and Karri forests since the early years of the colony, the expansion of settlement had been slow. Pastoral properties were sporadically occupied in the hinterland, but rapid development did not occur till late in the century. The first of the Western Australian gold strikes took place in the Kimberleys district of the far north, at Hall's Creek in 1885. It was short-lived but was followed by a number of other discoveries further south, the most important of the early finds being the Southern Cross field 200 miles east of Perth. Following the geologic trend eastward, the rich alluvial gold of Coolgardie was discovered in 1892, and in the following year was found the richest of them all, the Golden Mile of Kalgoorlie.

Prospectors and miners swarmed to these goldfields, as they had to those of Victoria and New South Wales. The population of Western Australia increased by 35,000 in 1896 alone. The improvement of the roadway and the building of a railway from Perth, along with the construction of a water supply pipeline from the Darling Scarp area to Kalgoorlie, quickened the pace of economic activity and made it possible to open up a vast area of farming and pastoral land between the coast and the goldfields. Settlers continued to push the farming frontier north and south from the railway line, and Western Australia's "wheat belt" developed rapidly. There were a number of other gold strikes in the central part of the colony, especially in the Murchison, Ashburton, and Pilbara districts; all were puny in comparison to the earlier discoveries, but each of the new fields stimulated settlement expansion. While pastoralists and farmers were spreading over the southern and central parts of the colony, pastoral occupance of the north (Kimberleys district) was also beginning. Cattle were overlanded to the Kimberleys for the first time in the 1880's and, despite several fierce setbacks due to such factors as cattle ticks and red-water fever, most of the grazing land was occupied by the turn of the century.

Railroads made an important contribution to both economic development and settlement expansion. The first short lines were constructed in the 1850's, and each colony continued a fairly rapid pace of railway building until there were over 10,000 miles of track in Australia as the twentieth century dawned. Unfortunately, the lines of the various colonies were unintegrated, with the result that different track widths were chosen, and the problem of non-uniform gauge has plagued Australia to the present day. Most of the major rail lines were designed to serve as gathering systems to funnel rural produce to the capital city. Thus they fostered the centralized growth of a single city in each colony, another pattern that has persisted.

Irrigation agriculture provided a further stimulus to settlement expansion. The first major schemes were developed in the Renmark-Mildura area of the middle Murray valley by the Chaffey Brothers beginning in the late 1880's. Most of the other irrigated farming areas in Australia are twentieth century developments. The largest scheme was in the middle section of the Murrumbidgee Valley (called the M.I.A.) in New South Wales, but there were numerous smaller developments, especially in Victoria and Queensland.

The six Australian colonies finally agreed to unite, and federation was achieved in 1901. At that time the total population of the new country was less than 2,000,000. The settlement pattern, however, was well developed; twentieth century additions have been mostly in the form of intensification rather than expansion into new areas.

Population Growth in the Nineteenth Century

Before proceeding to analyze the contemporary economic and social scene in Australia, it might be well to consider the origin of the population itself. From a pre-settlement total of 300,000 Aborigines and no Europeans, the population has grown to more than 12,000,000; less than 1 per cent of present-day Australians contain Aboriginal blood. The present population mix, then, is essentially the result of long-continued immigration, the pattern of which has fluctuated significantly through the years.

At first most immigrants were convicts who had been transported to Australia from England and Ireland for two reasons, to relieve overcrowding in British prisons and to supply cheap labor to the Austral colonies. That period of Australian history prior to the 1820's is generally referred to as the "transportation" era because it was predominantly a time of convict importation, with little governmental encouragement of free settlement. By 1821 the European population of New South Wales (which still included Van Diemen's Land and the Port Phillip District) was about 36,000; of these settlers, some 21,000 were convicts, 7,000 were emancipists (prisoners who had served their sentences and been freed), 1,500 were free settlers, and the remainder were children.

Transportation of convicts continued until 1868, amounting to a cumulative total of more than 160,000 prisoners during the eighty years of the practice, but the immigration of free settlers became increasingly important after 1821. Immigration totals fluctuated through the years, but the steady increase in total population (see Figure 3-2, pp. 52-53) is indicative of its continuance. Almost all of the migrants to Australia during the first half century were from the British Isles; indeed, New South Wales received essentially no immigrants who were not either British or Irish during this time. In South Australia the approach was different; the government encouraged Continental migrants, especially Germans, almost from the outset. By 1850 more than 4,000 Germans had come to South Australia, although these amounted to less than 10 per cent of the colony's population. Germans also began to immigrate to the Port Phillip District in the late 1840's.

During the latter half of the nineteenth century the population of Australia increased from 400,000 to 3,700,000; natural increase (excess of births over deaths) amounted to less than 60 per cent of the increment, whereas net immigration (excess of immigration over emigration) accounted for more than 40 per cent of the growth. During this time of significant total expansion there were also major changes in the composition of the population. The British or Irish origin of most of the immigrants continued to be dominant, but its proportion declined, and several other sources became important. Germans comprised the largest non-British element, settling in all the colonies in considerable numbers. Chinese also were notable at this time; they entered the eastern colonies in great numbers to participate in the gold rushes, and Chinese-born immigrants actually outnumbered German-born immigrants from the 1850's until the 1880's.[1] In the 1870's and 1880's a more diverse pattern of European minorities began to arrive in Australia as a result of Scandinavian and Italian migration. In addition, several tens of thousands of kanakas were brought into Queensland to work in the cane fields during this period.

By the turn of the century, the nonindigenous population of the country was 75 per cent Australian-born, ranging from about 80 per cent in Tasmania to about 70 per cent in Queensland. Another 20 per cent of the total had been born in the United Kingdom; mostly in England, many in Ireland, some in Scotland, and a few in Wales. The non-British 5 per cent of the population was proportionately declining at this time; Chinese were decreasing rapidly, Germans and Scandinavians more slowly, and Italians were continuing to increase, heralding the expanded immigration from southern Europe that marked the twentieth century.

Population Growth in the Twentieth Century

With the beginning of the twentieth century came federation of the colonies and a new outlook for the country. Net immigration, however, which had been on a downward trend for two decades, reached a negative value (i.e., a net emigration figure) for the first time in history, in part reflecting repatriation of kanakas and emigration of Chinese. The new states once again emphasized British immigration, and each of them produced policies for assisting British migrants. The migrant flow soon began to increase rapidly once again, and reached a total in excess of 130,000 per year just before the outbreak of World War I.

The war effectively stopped all immigration to Australia for half a decade, but the postwar period was one of migration acceleration. Net immigration totals increased to an annual average of about 40,000 during the 1920's. The migrants were primarily British; in most years fewer than 15 per cent were from continental Europe, largely Germany, Scandinavia, and Italy.

The depression years of the 1930's were marked by reduced migration movements, and early in the decade there was a long period of net emigration from Australia. After 1936 immigration increased, and for the first time migrants from continental Europe outnumbered those from the British Isles. Once again, however, the flow pattern was interrupted by a world war, and migration was at a virtual standstill from 1939 till 1945.

---

[1] Approximately 95 per cent of the Chinese immigrants were adult males.

Since the war there has been a continuing series of assisted migration schemes worked out between Australian state and federal governments on the one hand and various European countries on the other to foster and subsidize immigration. The result has been an almost continually rising immigration curve, although it should be pointed out that the emigration curve has followed the same trend at a lower level.

Slightly less than half the postwar migrants to Australia have come from the British Isles. The remainder have originated largely in southern and eastern Europe, although Germany and the Netherlands have also been major sources of supply. The largest number of non-British migrants have been Italians, comprising some 10 per cent of all postwar arrivals. Other significant nationalities represented, in addition to German and Dutch, are Polish, Greek, Yugoslav, Russian, Latvian, and Hungarian. In more recent years there has been an upturn in immigration from Malta, Spain, and Turkey as well.

The Contemporary Population of Australia

The demographic characteristics of Australia are unusual in a variety of ways. In the first place, it is striking that such a large country (sixth largest in the world) should have such a small population (forty-second largest in the world). We have discussed many of the environmental and historical reasons for this anomaly. The overall population density of the nation is less than four persons per square mile, easily the least of any significant country in the world.

Perhaps the second most notable feature of Australian demography is the centralization of its population; more than 57 per cent of the total population resides in the seven capital cities. Another 25 per cent lives in smaller urban areas, and less than 18 per cent can be classed as rural. There continues to be a slow increase in the proportion of each state's population found in its respective metropolitan area (the capital city of each state is considered to be a "metropolitan area," as is the national capital of Canberra). Such metropolitan centralization has been a long-established characteristic, as an historic holdover from the days of separate colonies, and it gives every evidence of persisting into the foreseeable future.

The general pattern of population distribution is a remarkable reflection of environmental influence. The drier parts of the continent are less productive than the wetter parts for the primary industries (farming and pastoralism), and are therefore sparsely populated. The humid, mid-latitude areas permit more productive use of the land and are occupied in moderate density. The only areas of high density settlement are urban. Thus the generalized pattern of population distribution shows an arc of moderate density extending around the southeastern coast from Rockhampton (Queensland) to Whyalla (South Australia), with the principal concentrations between Newcastle (New South Wales) and Geelong (Victoria). The major urban centers punctuate this arc as nodes of high density, but there are also areas of sparseness, such as the Australian Alps in

New South Wales and Victoria. Beyond the arc, moderate population density appears in the southeast and along the northern coast of Tasmania, in the southwest of Western Australia, and in various east coast valleys of Queensland. Most of the remainder of the continent, some 80 per cent of its area, is very thinly peopled.

A significant minority of the sparse population of the Australian inland consists of Aborigines. We noted earlier that the original indigenous population of perhaps 300,000 was severely decimated through the years, reaching a low point of about 40,000 at the beginning of the present century. Since that time the trend has been reversed, and the Aboriginal population has been increasing at a much faster rate than that of the nation as a whole. Only a few hundred Aborigines still maintain a primitive hunting-and-gathering existence; these inhabit the east central desert area of Western Australia. A tribal way of life is also carried on by a few thousand near-primitive, partially nomadic people in the northern parts of the continent, especially in Arnhem Land; they have frequent contact with civilization, however, and receive much of their food and clothing from government welfare stations and church missions. A far larger proportion of the Aboriginal population lives on the fringes of white society, holding jobs (especially as "cowboys" in the pastoral industry), occupying relatively permanent dwellings, and leading a sedentary existence; these are mostly half-caste or mixed blood people. Not all of the Aborigines live in the Outback, of course; in common with other Australians, they have joined the drift to the cities. Thus, most of the urban areas, except in parts of the Southeast and in Tasmania, include at least a few Aborigines among their citizenry. The total number of Aborigines in Australia in the late 1960's was slightly less than 150,000, divided about equally between full-bloods and half-castes. The former are found mostly in the Northern Territory, Queensland, and Western Australia, whereas the latter are more common in New South Wales and Queensland. The avowed policy of the government is to assimilate the Aborigine completely into Australian society; this will be a long and difficult process, but recent developments have been both progressive and enlightened.

In terms of the total population of Australia, the general rate of growth has been steady, but the actual annual increment has been slowly increasing (see Figure 3-3). Shortly after World War II the population of the continent was growing by about 100,000 per year; more recently it has been increasing by about 150,000 per year. This represents an annual growth rate of between 2 and 2½ per cent, which is similar to the average rate for the world as a whole, but is more rapid than that of most European countries. As the rate of natural increase is moderate, a major factor in population growth has been net immigration. This has amounted to an average of more than 80,000 persons per year since World War II. Thus, about 15 per cent of the total population represents "New Australians," immigrant arrivals since the war, amounting to nearly 2,000,000 individuals.

The population of Australia, then, is for the most part a relatively homogeneous blend—largely Caucasian, with a northwest European her-

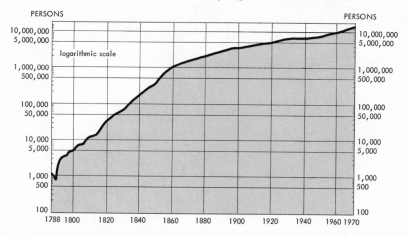

Figure 3-3   Population Through the Years

itage and culture; overwhelmingly Christian, comprised of about two-thirds Protestant and one-third Roman Catholic; linguistically simple, with almost everyone conversant in English even though it is not the mother tongue of some. This uniformity will probably decrease in the future, however, as the government pursues a policy of encouraging vaster and broader-based immigration. The rate of population increment can be expected to accelerate, and the diversity of the ethnic and cultural background of the newcomers can be anticipated to increase.

CHAPTER 4   *fruits of the land:*
the primary industries

We have seen that Australia is a vast land with a sparse population, situated in a relatively remote part of the world. It has a high standard of living and an advanced economy, both of which are based upon an abundance of resources, a skilled and energetic populace, and liberal infusions of Western technology and capital.

The Resource Base

At first glance the resources of Australia are somewhat less than impressive. The fundamental failing is a paucity of water, in both precipitation and stream flow. No other inhabited continent is so dry, and the influence of this aridity is clearly felt in the land-based primary industries. The arid milieu is conspicuously reflected in the landscape by the pattern of the natural vegetation. Forests are found in only a few areas, and there is a particular scarcity of softwoods. Lesser plant associations are dominant, and their presence emphasizes the negative aspect of the resource base. The soil resource comprises another problem; the prevalence of impoverished soils is accented by a lack of nutritive trace elements and an excess of salinity. Even the oceanic fishery has been unimpressive; despite the fact that fish comprise a minor part of the Australian diet, the country has been a net importer of fish products throughout its history.

There is, however, another side to the coin, and the brighter aspects of the resource base are becoming increasingly evident. First and foremost is the abundance and diversity of minerals of economic value. Probably only two other countries in the world, the U.S.A. and the U.S.S.R., possess a quantity and variety of ores greater than that of Australia. Indeed, Australia is among the world's leaders in output of every major industrial mineral except petroleum and natural gas.

Three other felicitous aspects of the Australian resource picture are forage, soils, and fisheries. A continent with limited forests is likely to have extensive areas of grass and shrub that can support a grazing industry. Such is the case in Australia, where the superb natural forage value of such species as Mitchell grass, saltbush, bluebush, and some types of spinifex has been augmented by the introduction of a number of exotic pasture grasses. Although Australia's soils are not notably fertile, many of them are quite responsive to the addition of chemical fertilizers, especially phosphate and various trace elements, which have raised productivity levels significantly in many areas. Only in the last few years has there developed an appreciation of the potential fishery resources in the seas surrounding Australia. While not yet exploited with much élan by the domestic fishing industry, the results of ingenious exploitation by foreign fishermen have not gone unnoticed, and there is considerable indication that fisheries will play a more important role in the economy and diet of Australia in the future.

In a spacious land with an uneven endowment of natural resources and a small population, the "development" of these resources is a matter of great concern, and judicious application of the relatively limited amounts of investment capital is called for. Nevertheless, development schemes, financed in both the public and private sectors of the economy, have been advanced on many fronts. The impoundment and diversion of surface waters has attracted most attention in the past, and will continue to loom large in the plans of resource developers at all levels. The most conspicuous of these efforts has been the Snowy Mountains Scheme, a billion-dollar project to divert the waters of two east-flowing rivers (Snowy and Eucumbene) into the west-flowing River Murray system for the purpose of hydroelectricity generation and increased irrigation usage. This twenty-five-year project is being completed on schedule, and, although its cost-benefit ratio is questionable, it has become a national status symbol of utmost significance. Soil improvement by mineral application has provided a less spectacular but no less impressive expression of resource development. For example, the fertile South Australian farming area now called Coonalpyn Downs was known prior to the 1950's as the Ninety Mile Desert, but minute additions of zinc and copper to the soil transformed an unproductive region into a major producer of grains, wool, and fat lambs. Forage improvement has also yielded fruitful results; notable projects currently under way include the large-scale eradication of brigalow scrub (*Acacia harpophylla*) in areas of central and southern Queensland to promote the growth of more nutritious forage, and the widespread cultivation of Townsville lucerne (*Stylosanthes humilis*), a legume of South American origin that has increased cattle carrying capacity by more than 500 per cent in several sections of Queensland. Another important botanical immigrant has been the exotic softwood; Australia has no indigenous pines (*Pinus* spp.), but a number of Northern Hemisphere pines have been established in plantations in various localities, giving rise to both lumber and pulp industries of significance. These are but a few examples of resource development projects, representing a field of endeavor that continues to occupy much attention among Australians. The country is fortunate in having a well-established federal research organization, the C.S.I.R.O. (Commonwealth Scientific and Industrial Research Organization), which has been a world leader in applying the results of scientific research to the solving of practical resource development problems.

Extractive Industries

MINING: DYNAMISM FOR TODAY AND TOMORROW. The extraction and processing of minerals has been a major factor in the economic development of Australia, almost from the time of earliest European settlement. A wide variety of minerals is found in commercial quantities, and some have been exported in volume. The total complement of mineral resources gives Australia an attractive base for industrialization. Furthermore, the establishment of mining centers, often in remote localities, has had a salutary effect on the spread of settlement, and some of the mineral strikes have sharply stimulated immigration into the country.

In recent years there have been fluctuations in mine output, mostly due to variations in world market prices. However, until the latter half of the 1960's employment in mining remained quite steady, with between 50,000 and 60,000 workers. The recent mineral boom changed all that, and despite the strong influence of mechanization, the number of people employed in mining has climbed significantly.

Coal has been the keystone of the mineral economy. It was the first mineral to be mined (in 1796) and the first to be exported (1801), and coal mining still employs about one-third of all the miners in the country. Every state except Tasmania has significant coal production, and Australia's total output of black coal (bituminous and subbituminous) gives it ranking among the top twelve countries of the world. Well over two-thirds of the output is from three areas in New South Wales: the northern coalfields in the lower Hunter Valley, the western coalfields inland from Sydney around Lithgow, and the southern coalfields in the vicinity of Wollongong (see Figure 4-1). These fields, approximately equidistant from Sydney, are the most significant in Australia from the standpoint of quantity, quality, and accessibility. Queensland ranks second among the states in both production and reserves; in recent years there has been rapidly increasing production, especially for export to Japan. In addition to the major uses of coal for heavy industry and railways, the generation of thermoelectricity provides a notable market for Australian coal. For example, essentially all of the commercial electricity in South Australia is generated from subbituminous coal, and most of Victoria's electricity is produced from enormous deposits of lignite (brown coal) in the Latrobe Valley, east of Melbourne.

If coal has been the keystone of the Australian mineral industry, *gold* has been the catalyst. As was mentioned in Chapter 3, early gold rushes in Victoria and New South Wales had a pervasive influence on the economy and settlement patterns of those two colonies, and the later strikes in Western Australia were equally important. Gold continues as a major

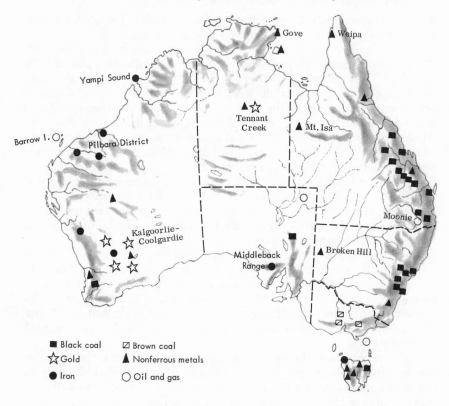

Figure 4-1 Major Mining Localities

mineral product, occupying nearly 10 per cent of the nation's miners and giving Australia fifth place among the world's nations in total output. More than four-fifths of gold mine production is from the Kalgoorlie-Coolgardie area of Western Australia, although considerable gold is also yielded as a by-product of base metal refining.

The mining of *nonferrous metals* is a more recent development in Australia, but much of the nation's reputation in mining has come from this branch of the industry. *Lead* and *zinc* ores normally occur together, and must be separated in concentrating plants; *silver* is usually produced as a by-product of the refining of lead and zinc. Australia is among the six leading world producers of all three of these minerals, with the bountiful ore bodies of Broken Hill (New South Wales) accounting for more than three-fourths of total output. The other major production center is

Mt. Isa (Queensland). *Copper* is also a major product from Mt. Isa, with several copper mining areas scattered in other states.

Historically Australia has been a moderate producer of *iron ore,* with steady output from the Middleback Ranges in South Australia and the islands of Yampi Sound in Western Australia providing a more than adequate supply for the domestic steel industry. However, a relaxation of ore export restrictions in the mid-1960's exposed a vast cornucopia of mineral deposits, especially in the Pilbara District of Western Australia. Almost overnight some of the world's largest reserves of iron ore were "discovered," and a frenzy of activity (developing mines, laying railway track, dredging new harbors, and building new towns) has transformed the somnolent Northwest into a boom region of great economic excitement.

Even more important from the long-run viewpoint may be the development of a *petroleum* and *natural gas* industry, which was completely lacking before the 1960's. Australia's first oil field was brought in near Moonie in southeastern Queensland in 1961; since then commercial production of oil has begun at several other localities, and the first commercial gas fields have been staked out in Bass Strait and in central Australia.

As overwhelming as the iron and petroleum discoveries have been, they are not the whole story. A varied storehouse of ores has been discovered recently, including the world's largest *bauxite* deposit (at Weipa, Queensland), and major reserves of *phosphate, zinc, nickel, copper, coal,* and *manganese.*

The mining breakthrough of the 1960's must rank with the introduction of Merino sheep and the development of refrigerated shipping as one of the most significant events in the entire economic history of Australia. And it is likely that more discoveries, perhaps *many* more, will be made before the activity subsides into a state of steady productivity.

LOGGING: LITTLE TODAY AND LESS TOMORROW.   It has already been noted that Australia is poor in timber resources because of the great extent of treeless areas and because of the limited varieties of timber available in those areas that are forested. Only about 2 per cent of the country is classified as "accessible" forest land; the comparable figure in the United States is 22 per cent. Almost all the indigenous timber cut in Australia is hardwood, the bulk of it eucalyptus. Exotic softwood plantations, largely of Monterey pine (*Pinus radiata*) from California, have been developed in every state; these somewhat assuage the acute shortage of native softwoods.

Each of the states has a timber industry of some importance, but the largest sawmill output is in New South Wales and Victoria. State forestry authorities impose strict limitations on timber harvest to insure that the annual cut does not exceed the annual growth increment. At the present writing, approximately 20 per cent of Australia's timber requirements must be filled by imports, mostly from Canada, the United States, New Zealand, and Malaysia. As domestic demand multiplies in the future, it is likely that the proportion of imported lumber will increase to 30 per cent, or even more.

FISHING: AN UNREALIZED POTENTIAL. Although Australia has traditionally been oriented toward the sea for its commercial links with the world, relatively little attention has been paid to maritime fishery resources until recently. Fish have been unimportant in the diet of most Australians, and there has been little attempt at export of fishery products. For the most part, the function of the fishing industry has been to supply fresh fish to the local metropolitan markets, and the only important fishery exports have been those (such as mother-of-pearl, pearl shell, and trochus shell) derived from the mollusc fisheries in the tropical waters off northern Australia.

This pattern began to change during the 1950's, when an important tuna fishery in southern waters began to be exploited, especially off the coast of South Australia. Further diversity was introduced in the 1960's with the rapid development of a crayfish (lobster) industry off Western Australia; the export of frozen cray tails to the United States burgeoned into an important source of foreign exchange. Under the stimulus of investment and expertise from Japan, cultured-pearl fisheries have been initiated in more than a dozen sheltered bays of the north coast; commercial oyster farming is carried on in several localities along the coast of New South Wales; and an expanding prawn fishery is being developed in a number of places.

The government attitude toward commercial fishing has become more aggressive in recent years, catalyzed by the continued successes of Japanese and Russian fishermen off the Australian coast. The proclaimed limit of territorial waters has been extended from three to twelve miles offshore, and more financial and legal help has been granted to the fishing industry. Even so, it should be kept in mind that fishing holds only a minor place in the Australian economy; for example, the total number of people employed in commercial fishing is less than the number of lead-zinc miners in the country.

Agricultural Industries

Throughout its history Australia has been heavily committed to the agricultural sector of the economy, both crops and livestock. Even in the atomic age, with most Australians living in cities and the great bulk of the labor force employed in non-rural occupations, the "primary industries" continue to play an important role. The nation is almost self-sufficient in agricultural produce; the only farm products of significance that must be imported are tea, tobacco, chocolate, and coffee. More important, perhaps, is the fact that exports from the agricultural sector have always comprised more than 80 per cent of all exports from Australia, and they continue to do so today despite the increasing export of ores and ore concentrates.

CROP FARMING: A QUESTION OF MARKETS. Probably the most remarkable thing about farming in Australia is the limited portion of the continent that is involved. Only a small fraction of the land area has the proper combination of climate, terrain, and soils to permit crop growing, and that small area is very restricted in its location. The major agricultural zone, within which farming appears in discontinuous segments, extends around the southeastern margin of the country in the form of a crescent that is from 100 to 250 miles wide, with its northeastern extremity in the Darling Downs of southeastern Queensland and its western end on the Eyre Peninsula of South Australia (see Figure 4-2). There is a comparably placed, though smaller, region occurring as a northwest-southeast trending band on the subhumid margin of Western Australia. Smaller farming areas, some of which are quite significant, are found in:

1. Some of the coastal lowlands and river valleys of eastern Queensland, from Brisbane to Cooktown
2. The north coast of Tasmania
3. The southeastern portion of Tasmania
4. An area extending inland from Esperance on the southern coast of Western Australia
5. A limited area around Perth in Western Australia

Despite the relatively small amount of land devoted to crops, however, it is more than sufficient to supply the domestic demand for foodstuffs and fibers. Greater acreages could be made available for most types of farming if the market were larger. There are occasional crop failures, to be sure, but the prime determinant of total production is normally the ability of Australian produce to penetrate overseas markets.

Wheat. Wheat is easily the leading crop; it occupies nearly half of all the cropped acreage and accounts for nearly one-third of the total value of all crops. For the most part wheat is grown as a mixed farming enterprise, with sheep raising as the other important element. There is usually a distinct correlation between the acreage and relative market prices for wheat and wool; as the price for one goes up, the acreage devoted to the other is likely to be curtailed. Thus, high wheat prices encourage the farmer to sow more acres to that crop and decrease the acreage allotted to sheep pasturage, and *vice versa.*

The basic environmental association is with precipitation; most wheat production is on lands that are semiarid to subhumid. In Western Australia, South Australia, and most of Victoria wheat is grown in areas that receive between ten and twenty inches of annual rainfall, with the twenty-inch isohyet generally marking the seaward margin of the wheat belt. In New South Wales wheat is grown between the fifteen-inch and thirty-inch isohyets, and it is grown in areas of slightly higher rainfall totals in Queensland.[1]

[1] Students of American geography will note that wheat farming in this country occurs in areas of greater annual precipitation; the apparent discrepancy can be resolved by a consideration of winter precipitation totals. Wheat is a winter crop (entirely in Australia; mostly in the United States), which means that it is planted in the fall and harvested in early summer. The Australian wheat belt receives most of its annual rainfall during the winter (which is the growing season for wheat), whereas most American wheat is grown in areas that have a summer precipitation maximum. Thus, higher annual totals in the United States are offset by a greater proportion of winter rain in Australia, which generally equalizes the growing season rainfall in the two countries.

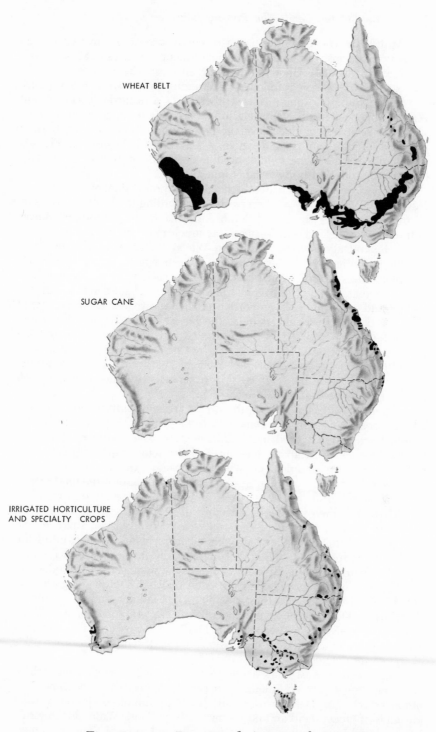

WHEAT BELT

SUGAR CANE

IRRIGATED HORTICULTURE
AND SPECIALTY CROPS

Figure 4-2   Principal Areas of Crop Farming

Australian wheat farming is an extensive operation, involving large farms with a relatively large capital investment, much use of machinery, and a relatively small labor requirement. In most wheat areas a four- to six-year rotation scheme is followed, alternating with pasture, other grains, and fallow. Superphosphate is used liberally as a fertilizer, and in recent years nitrogenous fertilizers have also been heavily used. Even so, average yields are relatively modest, normally between fifteen and twenty bushels per acre for the country as a whole. The Wimmera District of Victoria usually obtains the highest yields of all major producing areas, on account of its fertile soils and fairly reliable rainfall.

In most years the greatest acreage and production of wheat is in New South Wales, with Western Australia recording totals almost as large. Victoria is a strong third, and South Australia is also important. Wheat output in Queensland and Tasmania is much more limited.

A federal agency, the Australian Wheat Board, is in charge of all transportation and marketing arrangements for wheat. The government's five-year wheat stabilization plans (the fifth such plan began in 1968) provide a guaranteed price to the farmer for all wheat sold on the domestic market and a considerable proportion of the crop that is exported. Large export orders from China, Britain, the Soviet Union, Japan, and India stimulated record production during the latter part of the 1960's, but the long-term stability of these markets is not assured.

Other grains.   Two other winter cereals, oats and barley, are grown extensively in Australia, their combined acreage amounting to about 40 per cent that of wheat. *Oats* are a secondary crop grown throughout the wheat belt, as well as in some of the wetter areas in southeastern Australia where wheat is insignificant. Oats are a triple purpose crop; it is grazed by livestock, cut for hay, and harvested for grain. Eventually most of it is fed to livestock, with about one-fourth of the total crop being exported. *Barley* replaces or complements wheat in certain parts of the wheat belt, particularly in South Australia. Approximately one-third of the total crop is exported, one-third is fed to livestock, and one-third is malted or distilled.

There are three summer grain crops of significance. *Rice* output has increased dramatically in the last few years, with a large share of the crop exported to New Guinea and other Pacific islands. Almost all of the production is from New South Wales, especially in the irrigated districts along the Murrumbidgee River. Aspirations for significant rice production in tropical Australia have so far not been realized. Output of *grain sorghums* has also been increasing steadily. The leading production area is the Darling Downs section of Queensland. *Maize* (corn) is grown for grain in Queensland (especially the Darling Downs and the Atherton Tableland), and as a fodder crop associated with dairying in other parts of the eastern states.

Sugar cane.   Australia's leading specialty crop is sugar cane, which has been grown with considerable success for more than a century. It is produced on some 9,000 farms, mostly small, on the discontinuous coastal lowlands of Queensland and northernmost New South Wales. Cane growing is a highly mechanized activity, and, although several thousand itinerant cane cutters help bring in the harvest each year, the bulk of the crop is now harvested with machines. Much more cane could be grown with comparatively little effort, but the vagaries of the international market inhibit incautious expansion. Production quotas, as well as prices, are tightly controlled by the Queensland Sugar Board, which handles all marketing arrangements. Since the 1960's, when Cuba lost much of its international market for sugar, Australian production has increased significantly. Australia is now one of the five leading cane producers in the world, and is second only to Cuba as a sugar exporter, with major sales to the United States, Japan and the United Kingdom. Nevertheless, the international market is not firm, the Sugar Board has needed large loans from the federal government, and the Australian sugar industry is watching with hopeful caution the results of the 1968 International Sugar Agreement.

Horticulture. The intensive growing of fruits and vegetables occupies only about 1 per cent of Australian cropland, but comprises nearly one-fifth of total crop value. The output of almost every horticultural crop could be expanded considerably if there were markets available. Each state has an *apple*-growing area in a temperate climate zone near the capital city; most apple exports emanate from Tasmania, where apples are a major crop. Other deciduous fruits, especially *pears, peaches,* and *apricots*, are notable crops in various irrigated valleys, particularly those of the Murray, Murrumbidgee, and Goulburn rivers. Much of the output of these fruits is canned or dried for export. *Oranges* are grown on sandy soils, usually under irrigation; major areas of production are the Gosford district just north of Sydney, the Murrumbidgee irrigated areas, the Murray irrigated areas, and the hills around Perth and Adelaide.

Two tropical fruits are produced in large volume along the east coast and in much smaller quantity near Carnarvon on the west coast. *Pineapples* are grown for canning in the hills abutting the coast of southernmost Queensland, close to Brisbane. *Bananas* could be grown widely in the high-rainfall areas of coastal Queensland, but most production is concentrated along the extreme north coast of New South Wales, which is the southernmost area having sufficiently warm weather to raise bananas and still be close enough to the large urban markets of Sydney and Melbourne to supply them without much spoilage of the fresh fruit.

Most *vegetables* are grown in market gardening situations near the larger urban centers, to take advantage of the local market for fresh produce. In many cases the soils in such localities are only moderately fertile, but hard work and the use of fertilizers make them productive. *Potatoes*, on the other hand, need a cool, moist environment, so they are mostly grown in Tasmania and the cooler parts of Victoria, although there have been significant recent acreage increases in New South Wales.

Viticulture. There is a notable amount of grape growing in Australia, much of it dating from the early days of settlement. Only about 10 per cent of the crop consists of table grapes; the balance is evenly divided between wine and drying varieties. The South Australian vineyard areas, of which the most important is the Barossa Valley north of Adelaide, emphasize grapes for wine and brandy. The irrigated areas of the Murray and Murrumbidgee valleys specialize in varieties that can be dried into raisins, sultanas, and currants.

Nonedible crops. Two specialty crops are becoming increasingly notable in Australia. Production of *cotton* has demonstrated a remarkable increase in recent years; it is anticipated that Australia will be self-sufficient in most varieties by the early 1970's. Many areas are environmentally well suited to cotton growing; all important cotton areas utilize irrigation. The Namoi district of New South Wales, where production was initiated by immigrants from California, is easily the most important; another area of great interest, but one that faces overwhelming transportation handicaps, is the Ord River district of Western Australia, where immigrants from Arizona have been instrumental in the development of the cotton industry. Australian *tobacco* growers receive favored government treatment in that there are laws requiring that domestically manufactured cigarettes contain a continually increasing proportion of domestically grown tobacco. Principal production areas are in Queensland (especially the Atherton Tableland and the lower Burdekin Valley) and Victoria (especially the Ovens Valley), where "New Australians," particularly Italians and Albanians, are the principal growers.

SHEEP RAISING: DOMINANT RURAL INDUSTRY. Despite Australia's diversified crop production, animal husbandry has always been more important than farming. Livestock products normally are worth about three times as much as all crops combined in any given year, and the sheep is the source of about three-fifths of the value of all livestock products.

Ever since the early days of settlement the Australian economy has been said to "ride the sheep's back." Farming was difficult in the sterile sandstone hills around Sydney, and the early colonists soon turned to sheep raising as a source of income. In fact, most exploration outward from Sydney and other coastal settlement nodes was at least partially motivated by the desire to find more and better sheep pasturage. The emphasis has always been on wool production, so most of the early sheep imports were varieties of Merino. The present-day Australian Merino has been bred from Spanish, South African, English, French, and German stock, and it differs considerably from its ancestors. It is relatively large-framed and hardy and has proved to be adaptable to an arid climate as well as to high and low extremes of temperature. About three-fourths of all the sheep in Australia are Merinos.

Australia contains about fourteen times as many sheep as it does people, the total of nearly 170,000,000 amounting to 17 per cent of all the sheep in the world. Australia's wool output is 30 per cent of the world total, which is more than twice as much as the second-ranking producer. Although sheep raising has been tried wherever conditions held out any hope for success (and in many places where they didn't), most Australian sheep are found in the southeastern and southwestern portions of the country, generally in a broad crescent along and inland from the "wheat belt." The greatest concentrations are in New South Wales (more than 40 per cent of the total), where sheep raising dominates the rural scene almost everywhere except within fifty miles of the coast. Western Australia, Victoria, and Queensland each have about one-sixth of the Australian sheep population; South Australia and Tasmania have smaller numbers; and there are almost no sheep in the Northern Territory.

Extensive wool production. There are three basic types of sheep raising operations, of which the most widespread is the extensive pasturing of Merinos for wool production. As is seen in Figure 4-3, this type of operation occupies broad areas in the interior of Queensland, New South Wales, South Australia, and Western Australia. Large landholdings are typical, ranging in size from only 1,000 acres in better-watered areas to more than 1,000,000 acres in drier regions. Carrying capacity is low; in some cases, as many as 25 or 30 acres are required to support one sheep, and provision of watering points is essential.

These extensive properties, called "stations," usually breed their own stock, maintaining a nucleus of stud rams along with large numbers of ewes. The sheep are allowed to shift for themselves within large fenced pastures ("paddocks") most of the time. They are rounded up ("mustered") once a year, usually in fall or winter, for shearing, which is accomplished by an itinerant shearing team in a shearing shed that is often the most imposing building on the property. On the larger and more remote stations the annual shearing muster is the only time during the year when the entire flock ("mob") is brought under systematic scrutiny. On smaller and more heavily stocked properties, however, there may be other musters, at which time the animals are given such special care as jetting or dipping to combat ticks and inhibit flies.

Although the continent is unusually free from diseases that affect sheep, the stockman must contend with a number of other environmental problems. *Drought* is the most notable, of course; extended periods without rain cause both a decline in lambing percentages and an actual die-off in adult sheep, because on these extensive stations it is impractical to give the animals special care and they must prosper or decline on the basis of their ability to cope with nature. *Parasites,* both internal and external, sometimes cause significant problems. *Vermin,* comprising animals that compete with sheep (such as kangaroos and rabbits) or prey on sheep and lambs (such as dingoes and foxes), play a leading role in Australian demonography. Extraordinary efforts have been expended to eliminate them from sheep areas, including the construction of tens of thousands of miles of rabbit and dingo fences.[2]

Mixed sheep and grain farming. Throughout the wheat belt there are many properties that produce both crops and livestock products for sale. More than half of all Australian sheep are found in such situations. Wool and wheat are the principal products from these farms, but barley and oats are also raised in considerable volume, and the farmer sometimes emphasizes the output of meat (lamb or mutton) rather than wool.

[2] One dingo barrier fence extends unbroken through three states for more than 5,300 miles.

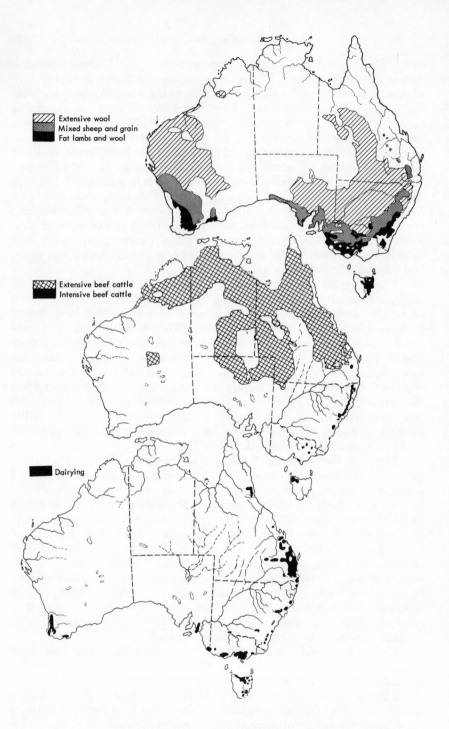

Figure 4-3 Dominant Types of Animal Husbandry

Sheep are more closely supervised and better cared for in areas of mixed farming, as both the size of the property and the number of animals are usually much smaller. In normal times there is a considerable movement of sheep from the extensive wool areas into the mixed farming zone. This involves the surplus stock from the wool properties, and mostly consists of old ewes and wethers. The farmer can take these animals and obtain a wool clip, then fatten them for sale, or sometimes breed them to produce fat lambs to sell.

Fat lamb production. The third principal type of sheep husbandry involves the production and fattening of lambs to sell for meat. Coarse wool (non-Merino or shorter wool) is usually a by-product of these operations. This is a fairly intensive form of pastoralism, involving improved, high quality pasturage. As demonstrated in Figure 4-3, the fat lamb areas are in the moister southeastern and southwestern corners of the continent, as well as in Tasmania. Better meat producing varieties of sheep, such as the Polwarth (a breed developed in Australia), Leicester, Suffolk, and various crossbreeds, are used.

BEEF CATTLE: INCREASING IN THE OUTBACK. The early development of beef cattle was not as widespread as that of sheep. Generally beef cattle raising has been developed in areas not suitable for the more profitable sheep raising and dairying, although beef cattle are an adjunct to both in moister country. In the northern portion of the continent there was a more distinctive and clear-cut development of cattle raising. Western and much of northern Queensland had become cattle country by the 1860's, and there was substantial cattle interest in the following decade in the Northern Territory. Cattle raising got started in northwestern Australia in the 1880's, with the overlanding of big mobs all the way from Queensland to the East Kimberleys.

In normal times there are between 13,000,000 and 14,000,000 head of beef cattle in the country. The extensive raising of cattle is the dominant land use throughout the monsoonal north, in much of central Australia, and in most of eastern Queensland. In addition, more intensive breeding and fattening of beef cattle is carried on significantly in many parts of eastern.Queensland and northeastern New South Wales. Statewide distribution shows that nearly half of all beef cattle are found in Queensland and nearly one-fourth are in New South Wales, with considerably smaller totals in the other states and the Northern Territory.

Intensive breeding and fattening areas are mostly in hilly tracts on the coastal slopes of southeastern Australia. The cattle are often run in conjunction with some other type of farm operation, such as fat lamb raising or crop growing. The pastures normally are "improved"; that is, the woodland or bush has been cleared and exotic grasses have been planted. This permits a denser pattern of stocking and a much higher rate of turnoff of marketable animals. Most of the beef that is produced in the more intensive areas is sold on the domestic market.

The extensive cattle areas, on the other hand, are oriented toward the export market, and most abattoirs are in coastal towns from which the chilled or frozen meat can be shipped directly overseas. Many of the stations, especially in the far north, do no fattening at all and simply function as breeding areas. However, most cattle stations in the extensive area also provide some fattening facilities, in the form of either improved pastures or supplementary feeds, so that the animals only must be "topped off" for a brief period on better feed before slaughtering.

Cattle are usually mustered twice a year, once for branding the new crop of calves and once for selecting the animals to be sold. The rest of the year they fend for themselves. Shorthorns and Herefords are easily the favorite breeds, and a cross between the two is commonplace; Brahmans and Santa Gertrudis are becoming increasingly popular and are sometimes used in crossbreeding.

The properties in the extensive area are mostly quite large, and, although the legendary 12,000-square-mile stations of the past have now been subdivided, there are still several that encompass more than 5,000 square miles each.[3] Most cattle stations, then, require a number of full-time employees to handle the many chores associated with such vast enterprises. Throughout the north and interior most of the hired hands are Aborigines, as it is becoming increasingly difficult to find white Australians who are willing to undergo the privations of a wage earner's life on a remote station. The psychological isolation of station life in the Outback has been eased considerably, however, by the universal use of three related amenities—the wireless transceiver, an inexpensive sending-and-receiving radio set that is available to every homestead; the Flying Doctor Service, which supplies medical advice by radio and medical attention by airplane; and the School of the Air, which provides every school-age child with correspondence lessons and daily radio contact with his own teacher.

The beef cattle industry of Australia has been undergoing considerable, if erratic, expansion in recent years. Much of this growth has been the result of expanding export markets in the United States and Japan. However, a number of technological improvements—vastly improved roads ("beef roads") to permit truck transport of marketable cattle from station to railhead, development of more nutritious pasture species, upgrading of cattle breeding, construction of export meatworks in hitherto unserved areas, and the liberal infusion of investment capital (especially American)—have also provided growth stimulus.

OTHER TYPES OF LIVESTOCK. There are some 5,000,000 *dairy cattle* in Australia, mostly found in the high rainfall country of the east coast. More than one-third are in Victoria, about one-fourth each in New South Wales and Queensland, and the other three states each have about 5 per cent of the total. The optimum environment for dairying (cool, moist climate with a long growing season) is about the same as that for fat lamb raising, so these two activities are frequently found in the same areas. The principal dairy breed is the Australian Illawarra Shorthorn (A.I.S.), which was developed in Australia and officially recognized as a distinctive

---

[3] For comparative purposes, the area of the state of Connecticut is just over 5,000 square miles.

breed in 1929; Ayrshires, Holsteins, Guernseys, and Jerseys are also common. Most dairy production is consumed locally, but a significant share is sent as milk or cream to a dairy factory for conversion into butter, cheese, or processed milk for export. The value of Australian butter exports is greater than that of any other agricultural products except wool, wheat, meat, and sugar. The dairy industry has been facing a price-cost squeeze of considerable magnitude, however, and is heavily subsidized by the government. The fifth successive Five-Year Dairy Stabilization Plan was begun in 1967, and the continuing protection of the industry has become a contentious political issue.

The number of *horses* in Australia is declining, as it is in most countries, but there are still about half a million. They are quite useful in the extensive cattle raising areas, so the great majority are found in Queensland and New South Wales. There is also considerable breeding of race horses in Australia; horse racing is the most popular sport in a very sports-conscious nation.

There are some 2,000,000 *swine* in Australia. Most are kept as an adjunct to general farming, but there are some specialized pig raising operations. Their numbers are increasing steadily. *Poultry* are widespread, but mostly raised on a small scale.

Irreverence for the Land

This brief survey of the primary industries has shown that some of the natural resources of Australia are bountifully bestowed, whereas others are much more limited in quantity, quality, or both. Despite this uneven endowment, the pattern of resource exploitation has been one of short-run expediency, with little thought to tomorrow's consequences. This is an expectable result when a relatively small number of immigrants invade a new and unspoiled continent; it has been characteristic of frontier settlements throughout human history. Yet the same pattern continues today, when Australia is no longer a frontier country. The population is still relatively small, and the land to be "conquered" is vast; thus frontier attitudes toward the land still prevail, although twentieth century techniques are brought to bear. The bulldozer becomes the deity, and the cloud of dust becomes the symbol of contemporary Australian civilization. "Development" of the land is important—some would call it essential; but development based upon exploitation without conservation is rapacious. The sorry spectacle of nineteenth century resource depletion in North America has been and is being repeated in Australia. In spite of the prominence of rural industries in Australian consciousness, there is little reverence for the land.

Much positive effort has been made in three general directions—impounding surface waters, tapping artesian aquifers, and enhancing soil productivity with fertilizers. However, most other aspects of the land resource have been subjected to shabby mistreatment, as suggested in these examples.

1. The unique fauna has been severely depleted. Game laws are few, market hunting is common, wildlife preserves are rare, and the use of poison is unbridled. Only when a species is threatened with extinction, as with the koala in the 1920's or the salt-water crocodile in the 1960's, does the government implement effective protection laws.
2. Australia is a land of few trees, and yet the practice of "ringbarking" (girdling the bark of a tree so that it dies) is very widespread in the eastern states. The idea is to replace the trees with grass so that there will be more pasturage for livestock.
3. Very little of the land is set aside as scenic preserves. There are several dozen areas called "national parks," but the great majority of them consist of only a few acres of bush surrounding some tennis courts. There is great need to reserve more lands of scenic value before they are despoiled.
4. Most incomprehensible of all, perhaps, is the massive overgrazing that is characteristic of most pastoral areas. Animal husbandry is the dominant rural industry of the nation, yet many thousands of acres have been denuded and eroded because of overstocking with sheep and cattle. The graziers are quick to blame drought and kangaroos for the problem, but objective studies have shown that the critical factor is usually overgrazing.

It is encouraging to note that a conservation movement is beginning to bestir. There were a few pioneers in wise use of resources in earlier years, but it was not until after the midpoint of the twentieth century that conservationists began to organize, effective publications began to appear, and governments began to take a slight interest in broad matters relating to conservation. These beginnings of a conservation movement are small, but they provide some rays of hope that "the lucky country" will not deliberately spoil its resource birthright. There is still time.

CHAPTER 5 *the modern*
civilization of australia

Most non-Australians have a mental image of the continent Down Under as a land of vast, dusty plains inhabited by hordes of sheep and kangaroos and peopled by hard-working, weatherbeaten country folk. This stereotype is enhanced by much of the literature of Australiana, which pays tribute to the "sunburnt land" and the hardy pioneers who occupy it. Such an image has validity in an areal sense, for most of Australia is both semiarid and rural, and the four-legged inhabitants are much more numerous than the two-legged ones. However, in respect to the Australians themselves, the stereotype is patently false. The people are overwhelmingly urbanites, the society is one of the most affluent in the world, the way of life is sophisticated and modern, and the economy is highly industrialized.

Australia's Urban Milieu

The typical Australian breadwinner lives in a suburban section of a large city, works five or five and one-half days per week in a factory, office building, or store, and commutes to his job in his own automobile. In his general pattern of life he is much like the typical American. Thus it comes as no surprise that 84 per cent of the Australian population is classified as urban, whereas the corresponding figure for the United States is 72 per cent.[1] Urbanism is clearly a dominant feature of the social geography of Australia.

CENTRALIZATION. Even more striking is the concentration of the urban population in a handful of large cities. Only seven cities in Australia

---

[1] These two statistics are only roughly comparable, for in Australia towns with more than 1,000 population are classed as urban places, whereas in the United States an "urban place" must have a population of at least 2,500.

are classified as "metropolitan"; these are the six state capitals and the national capital. These metropolitan urban areas contain 57 per cent of the continent's population, whereas the approximately 400 smaller cities and towns include some 27 per cent of the citizenry. In no other significant nation is the centralization of population so marked.[2]

Table 5-1. Centrality of Australian Population, by States

| | State | | | | | |
Proportion of Population	N.S.W.	Vic.	Qld.	S.A.	W.A.	Tas.
In capital metropolitan area	58%	66%	43%	67%	60%	32%
In other urban areas	29	20	34	16	17	38
Classed as rural	13	14	23	17	23	30

Table 5-1 illustrates the primacy of the capital city in each of the states. In four of the six states the majority of the population resides in the metropolitan capital, ranging from a high of 67 per cent in South Australia to a low of 32 per cent in Tasmania. Such capital city dominance has been pronounced in Australia since the earliest days of settlement. We saw in Chapter 3 that the settlement of each of the Australian colonies was initiated at a coastal location that was sooner or later proclaimed the seat of government for the colony. These settlement centers, then, had the early dual advantage of being both principal port and administrative headquarters for their respective colonies. This led directly to their development as leading commercial centers as well, with the fundamental benefit of an early start. In logical fashion, the land transportation patterns of the various colonies radiated outward from the capital focus. The growing population provided an increasingly large market and labor supply, which attracted secondary industries to the capital cities. Thus almost the full range of economic advantages was concentrated in the metropolitan centers, and the agglomerative tendencies continued through the decades. In New South Wales, Victoria, South Australia, and Western Australia the capital cities are located in the approximate centers of the settled areas; their position reinforced their significance as primate cities of these states. In Queensland and Tasmania the metropolitan cities are off center, making it easier for other cities to grow to relative importance, and in these two states the capitals contain a significantly smaller proportion of both population and urban economic activities.

THE URBAN HIERARCHY.   The urban hierarchy is clearly dominated by the capital cities (see Table 5-2). Sydney and Melbourne are metropolises ranking among the fifty largest cities in the world. The four other state

[2] For comparison, the seven largest metropolitan areas of the United States contain 20 per cent of the national population. Analogous statistics include Canada, 35 per cent; United Kingdom, 23 per cent; Japan, 21 per cent; West Germany, 14 per cent; and Soviet Union, 7 per cent.

capitals (Adelaide, Brisbane, Perth, and Hobart) are of much less international repute and national stature, but they demonstrate notable primacy in their respective states. Hobart is only twice as large as Launceston in Tasmania, but in the other states the capital city is strikingly larger than any other urban area. The ratio ranges from 10:1 in New South Wales (Sydney: Newcastle) to 37:1 in South Australia (Adelaide: Whyalla).

Medium-sized cities are scarce (see Figure 5-1). Below the level of the state capitals, there are only four cities with populations exceeding 100,000: Newcastle, Wollongong, Canberra, and Geelong. Smaller cities are somewhat more numerous; there are ten in the size range between 40,000 and 75,000, most of which function as important regional commercial centers. Fourteen towns are in the 20,000–40,000 class, and another three dozen have between 10,000 and 20,000 inhabitants.

In the states of New South Wales, Victoria, South Australia, and Western Australia a "typical" Australian urban hierarchy has developed. The capital dominates the life of the state; metropolitan population centralization ranges from 58 to 67 per cent of the total. Secondary cities are much smaller, and within various size categories they are scattered more or less equidistantly from the capital, apart from a few specialized mining or smelting towns. Small towns are also dispersed concentrically inland from the capital.

In Queensland and Tasmania the patterns are more exceptional. The former state has an extensive coastline along which there are discontinuous patches of productive agricultural land extending for a thousand miles northward from the capital. Furthermore, the rural productivity of inland

Table 5-2.   Australia's Largest Urban Centers

Rank	Urban Center	Approximate 1970 Population
1	Sydney, N.S.W.	2,600,000
2	Melbourne, Vic.	2,300,000
3	Adelaide, S.A.	850,000
4	Brisbane, Qld.	850,000
5	Perth, W.A.	600,000
6	Newcastle, N.S.W.	270,000
7	Wollongong, N.S.W.	190,000
8	Hobart, Tas.	150,000
9	Canberra, A.C.T.	150,000
10	Geelong, Vic.	130,000
11	Launceston, Tas.	75,000
12	Ballarat, Vic.	70,000
13	Townsville, Qld.	65,000
14	Toowoomba, Qld.	65,000
15	Ipswich, Qld.	60,000
16	Rockhampton, Qld.	55,000
17	Penrith, N.S.W.	50,000
18	Bendigo, Vic.	50,000
19	Gold Coast, Qld.	50,000
20	Cessnock, N.S.W.	40,000

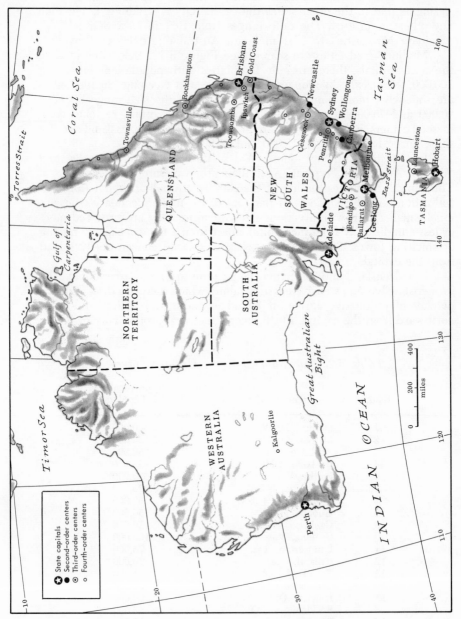

Figure 5-1 Principal Urban Centers

State capitals
Second-order centers
Third-order centers
Fourth-order centers

Queensland does not decrease uniformly with distance from the sea as is the tendency in the other mainland states. Hence, there is an irregular pattern of rural population and a decidedly unusual transportation network. Long railway lines extend inland from four ports situated at regular intervals along the coast, rather than being funneled toward the capital. Brisbane, then, contains only about two-fifths of Queensland's population, and other cities have a combined share that is almost as large. Truly autonomous regional urban nuclei have evolved more pronouncedly in Queensland than in any other state, due to the more scattered distribution of productive land and other resources, and the "corner" location of the capital.

The pattern in Tasmania is somewhat analogous to that in Queensland, but on a much smaller scale. Hobart, too, is off center, and it is distant from the fertile agricultural and pastoral lands of the north coast and the mining areas of the western mountains. Thus Hobart's share of the state's population is actually less than the cumulative total of the other Tasmanian urban areas. Furthermore, the proportion of rural population is higher in Tasmania than in any other state.

PRINCIPAL CITIES

New South Wales. Australia's largest metropolis and most cosmopolitan city is *Sydney.* The initial Antipodean settlement of 1788 was on the shores of Sydney Cove, a small indentation on the south side of Port Jackson Bay, which is only a stone's throw from the commercial core of present-day Sydney. The deep and sheltered waters of the bay were superb for ocean-oriented commercial purposes, but they are not as suitable for accommodating contemporary urban sprawl. There are a great many minor coves and other indentations that fragment the rolling site of the city and have given rise to a maze-like street pattern. Further, there is only one bridge across the long bay, and, despite the highly efficient ferry system, urban development on the south side of the bay is much more expansive than it is to the north. Sydney is the leading commercial city as well as the largest industrial center of the country. Nearly one-third of all Australian manufacturing is found there; the industrial structure is highly diversified, reflecting the national structure.

Newcastle and *Wollongong* are the state's secondary cities of note. Both are primarily centers of heavy industry, combining the advantages of coastal location and nearby coal fields. Most of Australia's iron and steel is produced in these two cities, and there is also great emphasis on metal fabrication and machinery production. Cities of third rank in New South Wales include *Penrith,* an industrial and market center at the foot of the Blue Mountains west of Sydney; *Cessnock,* a coal mining town in the lower Hunter Valley; *City of Blue Mountains,* a chain of resorts along the main transport route west of Sydney; and *Broken Hill,* the world famous mining town situated in splendid isolation in the arid west of the state.

Victoria. Australia's other world-class city is *Melbourne.* It was founded near the head of Port Phillip Bay as a nucleus to serve a pastoral hinterland. However, the Victorian gold rushes of the 1850's worked major changes on Melbourne. Prosperity in the hinterland (based on both mineral and agricultural productivity) combined with strict protective tariffs for local manufacturing to engender rapid urban growth. During the last half of the nineteenth century Melbourne was larger than Sydney, and for the first twenty-six years of this century it was the temporary capital of the nation, until Canberra was finally sited. The economy of Melbourne is oriented more toward commerce and finance than it is toward manufacturing; even so, it produces more than one-fourth of all Australian factory output. The industrial structure is well diversified, but there is particular emphasis on machinery, automotive, clothing, and shoe production.

Geelong, Australia's tenth largest city, is located on the edge of Port Phillip Bay some fifty miles southwest of Melbourne. It is an important industrial city, characterized by large factories and rapid recent development. Third echelon cities in Victoria are *Ballarat* and *Bendigo*, each located about seventy-five miles (west and northwest, respectively) from Melbourne. Both experienced major gold rushes, and both have persisted as important regional commercial centers, as well as attracting a considerable amount of secondary industry (especially textiles, clothing, and machinery).

Queensland. The capital city of *Brisbane* vies with Adelaide as Australia's third largest urban center. The city was founded on the navigable Brisbane River some ten miles inland from the coast. Brisbane was chosen as the capital of the new state of Queensland in 1859 and has been the leading city in the state ever since. The city occupies a rolling site on both sides of the river, spreading eastward to the sea and westward into the foothills of the Great Dividing Range. Its function is largely commercial, although it has notable industrial production in food processing, wood products, and certain types of machinery. The subtropical location of Brisbane invests it with a character rather apart from that of the other Australian metropolises.

As noted earlier, Queensland contains several smaller cities of considerable regional significance. *Townsville* and *Rockhampton* are the principal centers of the northern and central portions, respectively, of the state; they occupy similar situations in that both have fertile farmland nearby and both serve productive pastoral and mining hinterlands. *Toowoomba* and *Ipswich* are inland cities, the former functioning as commercial center of the fertile Darling Downs agricultural region, and the latter a long-established coal mining and farming center in many ways analogous to Cessnock in New South Wales. Located in the extreme southwestern corner of the state, *Gold Coast* is a rapidly growing seaside resort agglomeration with a national clientele.

South Australia. The focus of the planned colony of South Australia was *Adelaide*. It was laid out in a regular rectangular pattern on the narrow coastal plain between the Gulf of St. Vincent and the Mount Lofty Ranges. Its chief function has always been commercial, but it has also made a singular contribution to Australian industrial production, initially as a center for the farm machinery industry, and more recently in the output of automobiles, fabricated metals, and diversified machinery.

There are no second- or third-rank cities of significance in South Australia. *Elizabeth* is a government-founded industrial and residential center that dates from the mid-1950's; it was designed as a decentralized nucleus away from the capital city, but its location only fifteen miles from the commercial core of Adelaide predestined its absorption as a metropolitan suburb.

Western Australia. The capital of Australia's western state is in many ways the most isolated city in the world, some 1,400 air miles from its nearest urban neighbor. *Perth* is located on a broad reach of the Swan River some ten miles inland from the coast. It was the nucleus of a partially planned agricultural and pastoral colony whose prosperity received a significant boost with important gold rushes in the 1890's. Its economic structure is broadly diversified, as would be expected from its location. Perth's outport is *Fremantle*, which has extensive docking facilities in the mouth of the Swan River; just south of Fremantle on the coast is the rapidly-growing heavy industrial center of *Kwinana*.

The second largest urban area in the state is *Kalgoorlie*, the old mining town which has become the commercial center of the eastern goldfields; its population, however, is less than 25,000.

Tasmania. *Hobart* is the smallest of the state capitals. It was founded in 1804 as a supplementary penal colony on the southwest side of the broad estuary of the Derwent River. The city occupies gently sloping land between the river and the rocky sides of Mt. Wellington. Despite early prosperity, Hobart has generally experienced slow growth in comparison to the other capitals. It is a major apple shipping port, and it has a specialized industrial structure that emphasizes nonferrous metal smelting, wood products, and paper products.

The hub of Tasmania's north coast is *Launceston*, the largest of the third echelon cities in Australia. It is a port located at the upper end of the deep estuary of the Tamar River, some forty miles from the open sea. It is the principal Tasmanian port for Bass Strait shipping and is noted for the production of machinery and woolen textiles.

Northern Territory. Although more than 60 per cent of the population of the Northern Territory is classed as urban, there are only a few towns, and they are all small. The administrative center and only port of the Territory is *Darwin*. It is the principal trading town of the "Top End" and boasts an impressive jet-age airport, but the economy of Darwin is based mostly upon government payrolls and other expenditures. *Alice Springs*, situated close to the exact center of the continent, is an important regional trading town and tourist hub, despite its small size and remote location.

Australian Capital Territory. The confederation agreement of 1901 stated that the federal capital should be located in New South Wales, but at least 100 miles from Sydney. After a seven-year search, the location and boundaries of the A.C.T. were decided upon, and a six-year international competition for planning the capital was held. Construction began in the 1920's, and in 1927 the capital was officially moved from Melbourne to *Canberra*. It is a uniquely designed city whose planning and construction have been alternately criticized ("a good sheep station spoiled") and admired from many angles. In recent years it has been the fastest growing city in the nation, and much of the criticism has been replaced by praise as the federal capital (like the Snowy River Scheme) has become a sort of national status symbol.

The Economy: Sophisticated, Industrialized, Paradoxical

The Australian economic structure has all the characteristics of a modern, industralized nation. Primary activities employ only 12 per cent of the work force, with rural industries (agriculture, pastoralism) accounting for most of that total. Secondary activities (manufacturing) give employment to 26 per cent of the labor force. Tertiary activities provide the remaining 62 per cent of the employment, with the principal categories being trade, 16 per cent; services, 14 per cent; transportation, communications, and utilities, 11 per cent; government, 10 per cent; and construction, 9 per cent. Table 5-3 demonstrates the close correspondence between this structure and that of the United States.

Table 5-3. Australian and U.S. Economic Structures Compared

Major Economic Activities	Proportion of Work Force Employed	
	Australia	United States
Manufacturing	26%	28%
Trade	16	19
Services	14	17
Transport, Communications, Utilities	11	6
Agriculture and Pastoralism	10	8
Government	10	16
Construction	9	5
Other Activities	2	1

Even without a consideration of population distribution, then, it would be clear from these figures that the Australian economy is strongly urban-oriented. A high proportion of manufacturing, services, trade, construction, and government employment would logically be concentrated in cities and towns, as well as a somewhat smaller proportion of transportation-communications-utilities employment.

THE EXPORT PARADOX.   The principal paradox of the Australian economy is found in a consideration of export earnings. The rural industries, which provide employment for only 10 per cent of the work force, are the source of most of the nation's exports; other facets of the economy, which essentially means manufacturing in this case, provide a disproportionately small percentage of the exports. The export dominance of the primary industries is shown by the fact that in a typical year, raw primary products (such as wool, wheat, and ores) comprise nearly two-thirds of all exports, processed primary products (such as meat, sugar, and canned fruits) comprise nearly one-fourth of all exports, and manufactured goods other than primary products make up only about one-seventh of all exports.

Such a situation is a source of significant long-run insecurity for the economy. Primary product exports are notably vulnerable to international market variability, and thus to price fluctuations based on factors that are completely external to Australia. Furthermore, any internal calamity, of which by far the most pertinent is the frequency of drought, can invoke a sharp decrease on the supply side, resulting in a recessionary effect on the entire domestic economy. The recent history of Australia has demonstrated examples of the debilitating effect of both these factors (international demand and domestic supply) on several occasions. That such conditions have not been catastrophic in the past is no assurance that they will not be in the future.

AUSTRALIA AS AN INDUSTRIAL NATION. We have treated the rural industries in Chapter 4. It is worthwhile here to consider in some detail the manufactural sector of the economy.

Secondary industry developed in Australia under several handicaps, the most important of which was isolation. During most of its formative history Australia had to depend upon overseas factories, particularly in Britain, to supply the great majority of needed manufactured goods. This dependence upon a distant, and therefore relatively expensive, source has persisted to the present with regard to a continually decreasing but nevertheless significant variety of items. However, with the emergence of many types of domestic manufacturing, often a slow and tortuous process under the aegis of major protective tariffs, the basic industrial dependence upon foreign sources has taken a different turn. As Australian manufacturers become established, the limitations of the domestic market set relatively narrow margins for expansion. Thus, isolation is reflected as a market problem rather than a supply problem. The cultivation and exploitation of overseas markets by the Australian manufacturer is difficult and limits his opportunities for achieving economies of scale in production.

Protectionism played an important role in the historical development of manufacturing in Australia and is still significant for a few industries. Much of the early industrial lead in Victoria, for example, can be attributed in large part to a tariff policy that fostered the shoe and garment industries of Melbourne. After federation, the customs barriers between states were removed but were largely replaced by national restrictive tariffs. Protectionism may have been essential in the early years, but it does not foster dynamism in a more mature industrial nation. Furthermore, it encourages, or at least leads to toleration of, monopolies.

Monopoly, or tight oligopoly, is a significant characteristic of many industrial classes in Australia. In such basic industries as steel, cement, glass, paper, and sugar, production is entirely in the hands of a single, or of a very few, corporations. In some other types of manufacturing there is a quasi-monopoly at the state, rather than national, level. It has already been pointed out that the six colonies developed independently of each other, and in many ways the six states still form relatively discrete economic entities, a pattern fostered by their population distribution patterns and transportation networks. As a result, many industrial firms find it expedient to establish a factory in each capital city to serve the respective state markets.

A matter of some concern to Australian economists, and of even greater import to Australian politicians, is the degree to which foreign capital and foreign corporate enterprise have entered the Australian economy. This phenomenon is not restricted only to the manufacturing sector, of course, but it is particularly marked there. It is estimated that about one-third of all Australian manufacturing is foreign owned, often through subsidiaries established in Australia, and another 5 to 10 per cent is foreign controlled. Such considerable foreign investment in secondary industry is a mixed blessing, with the advantages of risk capital and technical competence and the disadvantage of possible economic colonialism. In the past, most overseas investment was from Britain; today the United States is the principal source, and Japanese investment is increasing.

The industrial structure of Australia is generally well diversified, reflecting the fact that Australian manufacturers supply most of the wide range of demands of the domestic consumer market. Table 5-4 portrays the contemporary industrial structure, as measured by employment in manufacturing. The principal types of manufacturing include the following.

Table 5-4.   Australian Industrial Structure

Major Classes of Manufacturing	Proportion of Total Manufactural Employment
Transportation equipment	13%
Food processing	12
Nonelectrical machinery	12
Electrical machinery	7
Textiles	7
Clothing	6
Primary metals	6
Fabricated metals	5
Wood products	5
Chemicals	4
Printing and publishing	4
Paper products	3
Other	16

Transportation equipment.   The automotive industry is the most important portion of this class of manufacturing. Auto making got an early start in Adelaide, where much of the actual manufacture of motor bodies is still carried on. Melbourne is the overall leader in production, however, especially in auto assembly. The industry is mostly composed of subsidiaries of American and British organizations, with the three principal producers being General Motors-Holden's, Ford, and Chrysler. Railway rolling stock and tramcar manufacture are mostly done in government owned factories in the capital cities, especially Sydney. Shipbuilding is accomplished mostly in private shipyards; the major shipbuilding center by far is the small South Australian port of Whyalla. Aircraft manufacturing is limited.

Food processing. This diverse class of manufacturing is widely dispersed over the settled parts of the continent. The larger flour mills are located in the capital cities, but smaller ones are scattered throughout the wheat belt. The three dozen raw sugar mills are concentrated in cane growing areas of Queensland, whereas the major sugar refineries are in the capitals. Meat packing plants tend to be market oriented, although a number of export abattoirs are situated in Queensland ports to expedite the direct overseas shipping of beef products. Fruit and vegetable processing is mostly accomplished in the horticultural districts, as in River Murray towns or near the capital cities. Dairy factories and breweries are mostly market oriented, thus concentrated in the larger cities.

Nonelectrical machinery. Although some specialized machinery is still imported from North America or Europe, most domestic machinery needs are satisfied by Australian producers. Generally speaking, the machinery industry is concentrated in Sydney and Melbourne, although there is increasing output in such smaller centers as Newcastle, Wollongong, Adelaide, and Brisbane.

Electrical machinery. This is a growing industry that is technically quite efficient. Most of the major production is by companies with overseas (especially U.K. and U.S.A.) affiliations. Two-thirds of the output comes from factories in Sydney, and most of the rest is produced in Melbourne.

Textiles. The emphasis of this industry is understandably on woolen textiles. There is some cotton textile production by a few large companies, but most light-weight cotton goods are imported. As with the clothing industry, Melbourne and Sydney dominate production.

Clothing. The knitted clothing and hosiery industries are well established in Australia, supplying most of the domestic demand. Other types of apparel are manufactured in smaller quantities. More than half the domestic output is from Melbourne; much of the rest is from Sydney.

Primary metals. There is a flourishing iron and steel industry that utilizes domestic materials, supplies almost all of the domestic demand, and is actively seeking to penetrate foreign markets. Major production centers are Newcastle and Wollongong, but there are new blast furnaces and steel mills at Whyalla and Kwinana. The principal nonferrous metal smelters and refineries are located either near the mines (as at Mt. Isa), or at logical tidewater sites (as at Pt. Pirie, S.A., where most of the Broken Hill ores are smelted), or near major electric power sites (as at Hobart).

As indicated by the preceding discussion, most Australian factories are associated with the major population concentrations. More than 90 per cent of all manufacturing is found within the crescent-shaped coastal zone between Rockhampton (Queensland) and Whyalla (South Australia), and the majority is agglomerated between Newcastle (New South Wales) and Geelong (Victoria). Indeed, secondary industry is even more concentrated in the metropolitan areas than population is; in the five mainland states the proportion of manufacturing located in the capitals ranges from a high of 85 per cent in Adelaide to a low of 55 per cent in Brisbane. Sydney and Melbourne are the largest industrial centers, of course, containing between them nearly three-fifths of the nation's factories. Secondary industrial nodes are much smaller. Only eight other cities have as much as 1 per cent of national industrial employment, ranging downward from 7 per cent in Adelaide through Brisbane, Newcastle, Perth, Wollongong, Geelong, and Hobart to 1 per cent in Ballarat.

TRANSPORTATION: CRITICAL AND COSTLY.   The basic geography of Australia is such that transportation needs and transportation problems are of primary significance. The land is vast, the population is sparse and concentrated in a few nodes that are great distances apart, the people are both mobile and affluent, much of the resource wealth (particularly mineral) is inconveniently distant from the populated districts, the export economy has long been dependent upon bulky primary products, and there are essentially no navigable inland waterways. Given this set of conditions, it is easy to see why Australians have paid much attention to the development of transportation.

The governments, federal and state, have taken a leading role in transport development, for the costs have usually seemed too great to entice much private investment. For example, Australia's early railroads were privately owned, but all of them developed such financial difficulties that they succumbed either to bankruptcy or government takeover. A significant portion of each government's contemporary budget is for transportation items, and nearly one-tenth of the Australian work force is employed in the transportation-communications-storage triad.

Roads.   It is physically less difficult and less costly to build roads in Australia than it is in many countries because much of the land is level and forests are uncommon. Nevertheless, a sparse population scattered over a vast land area calls for an extensive roadway network but does not provide adequate financial backing. Thus, Australia has more than 500,000 miles of roadway, but fewer than 10 percent of the rural roads are paved and less than two-thirds of the mileage is more than sporadically maintained. Even so, the roadway network in the settled parts of the southeast is fairly complete, and a high proportion of the mileage in the densely settled areas is paved, although only a tiny fraction of the mileage is more than two lanes wide.

Some 4,000,000 cars, trucks, and buses are licensed in Australia. Most of them are operated in the densely settled areas, putting a distinct strain on the roadway system in these localities. In contrast, the Outback roads are relatively undertraveled. Australia boasts the third highest per capita vehicle ownership of any nation, with 0.4 per cent of the world's population driving more than 2 per cent of the world's cars. Roadway transport moves about three-fourths of all domestic freight but accounts for only about one-third of all ton-miles hauled.

Railroads. Railway building got an early start in Australia, when the first short line opened in 1854 between Melbourne and its outport. For three decades railway expansion was desultory, but beginning in the 1880's the rail nets grew rapidly. Because settlement grew separately in independent colonies, the isolated and discrete railway systems developed. In each colony (except in Queensland and to a lesser extent Tasmania, where, as we have seen earlier in this chapter, atypical conditions prevailed) the railway net centered in the port-capital and was totally uncoordinated with the net in adjacent colonies. Even today only ten interstate border crossings are effected by rail lines.

The contemporary railroad pattern of Australia consists of six state-owned systems, as well as a federal system that operates the transcontinental line between South Australia and Western Australia and the two lines in the Northern Territory. The picture is further complicated by the use of different gauges (width between the rails) in different areas, another legacy of the separate colonial railway systems. The Victorian and most of the South Australian systems operate on wide gauge (5' 3"); the New South Wales and Commonwealth systems utilize standard gauge (4' 8½"); and the Queensland, Western Australian, Tasmanian, and portions of the South Australian systems use narrow gauge (3' 6"). Gauge rationalization by reconstruction to standard gauge has been accomplished on the main line from Melbourne to Brisbane via Sydney and is being completed on the transcontinental route from Sydney to Perth. However, the costs of such a project are so high that it is unlikely to be extended to other lines.

The role of railroads in Australia today is much the same as it was in the past, except that their relative significance has declined. Their principal function is still to funnel the primary products of a state to or through the capital city. As in most countries, the railways are best adapted to moving the large load on the long haul. The principal commodities carried are coal, other minerals, and agricultural produce. There is considerable competition with trucking lines for freight and with airlines for passengers. Railway freight haulage accounts for about one-fifth of all freight transported, whether measured by tons or by ton-miles. Freight traffic continues to expand modestly each year, whereas passenger traffic is suffering a small annual absolute decline.

In summary it can be said that the Australian railway systems are both efficient and significant. Nevertheless, it is fair to note that they operate at a financial loss. In most years only New South Wales shows an operating profit on railway operations, and even this profit evaporates if loan interests and other overhead are charged. In a normal year, the seven railway systems of Australia show a cumulative net financial deficit of from $10 million to $25 million.

Water transport. Inland waterway transportation has never been important in Australia. There was some steamboat traffic on the Murray-Darling system during the latter half of the nineteenth century, but railway competition put an end to that.

Coastwise traffic is of great significance to the economy. Although only about 5 per cent of all domestic freight travels by coastal steamer, long hauls are involved, amounting to about half of all ton-miles carried. Bulk products are the principal commodities handled; coal and iron ore make up more than half of the total tonnage, and other minerals, such as petroleum products and bauxite, comprise most of the remainder. Some 250 vessels are licensed for interstate or intrastate commerce. All are of either Australian or New Zealand registry, as these have legalized preferential position. Nearly half of all coastwise commerce is handled through the ports of Wollongong, Newcastle, and Whyalla, all of which are involved in the reciprocal flow of steel making materials.

Air transport. Australians travel more miles by air per capita than do people of any other country. This is a fairly straightforward result of widely separated cities, a high standard of living, and good flying weather.

The Commonwealth government set up a Civil Aviation Branch in 1921, with the initial goal of developing air service in Outback areas where other means of transport were lacking. Indeed, the first route was established between the remote towns of Geraldton and Derby in Western Australia. City-serving runs were not begun until the 1930's, although the nation is blanketed with scheduled routes today.

There is a three-fold hierarchy in contemporary Australian commercial aviation. (1) The only international carrier is Qantas Empire Airways, a government owned line that evolved from a small Outback company (Queensland and Northern Territory Aerial Services, whose initials are incorporated into Qantas) that began operating in 1922 and thus is claimed to be the second oldest air transport company in the world. (2) There are two domestic carriers with nationwide service. One is government owned and the other is private, but the government closely supervises both, so that even though they compete over essentially the same routes, their services and even their schedules are almost identical. (3) About a dozen smaller companies, most of them subsidiaries of the two national carriers, serve essentially as intrastate feeder lines. In general, Australian civil aviation service is efficient, relatively inexpensive, heavily used, and characterized by a remarkable safety record.

The use of aircraft in the Outback is also of great significance. Every pastoral property of any size has an airstrip, if only to accommodate emergency Flying Doctor Service. Air transportation of personnel and supplies is widespread, however, and such activities as seeding, fertilizing, and vermin control are often done from aircraft.

CHAPTER 6 the world
of the australians

Historically, Australia's world view has been necessarily narrowed by geographical isolation. She is half a world away from the mother country and is alienated by culture and custom from her Asian neighbors. Thus, Australians have generally, and understandably, been much more concerned with domestic affairs than they have with international events. The principal exception to this generalization has been in Australia's close liaison with Britain, which was the colonizing homeland, the source of most imports, the purchaser of most exports, and the paternalistic guide in foreign affairs. When Great Britain went to war, Australia loyally followed; the various Australian colonies supplied volunteer troops for the Boer War, Australia made a heavy commitment in World War I, and Australia was a strong participator in the European-North African-Middle Eastern portion of World War II long before Japan widened the conflict to the Pacific.

The close association with Britain engendered a filial relationship between Australia and other elements of the British Commonwealth. New Zealand, of course, shares Australia's corner of the world, and their mutualism is predestined. But Australia also has maintained ties with other parts of the "Empire," especially Malaysia, India, Ceylon, South Africa, and Rhodesia, and to a lesser extent with Canada, Pakistan, and Burma.

Australia has always been interested in the South Pacific. From the earliest days of settlement, Australian settlers urged a reluctant British Foreign Office to exert hegemony over various island groups. This course was not followed until France and Germany began colonial annexations in the Pacific in the 1870's. During the latter half of the nineteenth century Australians had cause to focus much attention upon Melanesian islands because of the large number of kanakas that were brought from such places as New Hebrides to work on Queensland sugar plantations. In addition, Australian interest in Papua and New Guinea has been of long standing; Papua's annexation by Britain in 1888 was a direct result of insistence by Australians.

Thus, it is incorrect to say that Australia has been unaware of, and uninterested in, world affairs. Indeed, it is a well-established business and professional policy in Australia to grant "long service leave" to responsible employees whereby they can go "overseas" (essentially, to the United Kingdom) for several months of stimulation after several years of employment in Australia. Nevertheless, Australia has been basically a remote and isolated land, and until almost the midpoint of the twentieth century she was relatively content to maintain her principal trade ties with Britain and to let Britain exert major guidance in her foreign policy.

Changing Policies in a Changing World

The great stimulus for modification of this pattern of isolationism was the Pacific phase of World War II, and the new trend was further strengthened by the changing international economic and political conditions of the immediate postwar era. During the last month of 1941 and the first few months of 1942 Australia was abruptly faced with the cold reality of imminent disaster and the realization that Britain could no longer provide protection. The military might of Japan overran Southeast Asia, including the East Indies, and penetrated New Guinea and the Solomon Islands. The British military bastions of Hong Kong, Singapore, and Rangoon were speedily conquered, and the backbone of the British Far Eastern Fleet (the battle cruisers *Repulse* and *Prince of Wales*) was destroyed in a single brief attack. The direct threat to Australia was emphasized by the repeated bombing of the north coastal towns of Darwin, Wyndham, Broome, and Pt. Hedland, and Sydney harbor was actually penetrated by Japanese mini-submarines.

The Japanese offensive toward Australia was finally stopped by a massive, three-pronged Allied effort that involved an American naval victory in the Battle of the Coral Sea, an American Marine Corps action on the island of Guadalcanal, and an Australian land and air victory in the Owen Stanley Mountains of New Guinea. Australia became the base from which the overwhelming Allied (largely American) counteroffensive was launched to reclaim the Pacific from Japan. As a result of this series of events, Australia was forced to reassess its historic diplomatic and military dependence upon Britain; the importance of alliance with the United States became undeniable.

The trend of postwar economic and military decisions in Europe has served to further weaken the ties between Australia and Britain. The latter's potential entry into the European Economic Community (Common Market), an avowed goal of the British government, would do away with the preferential treatment of Australian imports, and the British decision to withdraw its military presence from "east of Suez" by the early 1970's removes the last vestige of hope that Australia could rely on Britain for quick military assistance.

Australia's Contemporary International Relations

As disentanglement with Britain in diplomatic, military, and economic spheres continues, Australia is fostering an ever-increasing rapprochement with the United States on one hand, and with various Asiatic nations on the other. In matters of trade, the British share continues to decline, being replaced by trade relations with the United States, Japan, China, and other nations. An increasing proportion of Australian military equipment is being purchased from the United States, and Australian military commitment in Southeast Asia (specifically in Malaysia, Viet Nam, and Thailand) in the form of troops and "advisers" continues. The American alliance has become a cornerstone of Australian foreign policy, and diplomatic consultation with the United States has been accelerated. As with trade, Australian foreign aid has become strongly oriented toward Asia, as emphasized by participation in the admirable Colombo Plan and by the cementing of friendly relations with Indonesia, Australia's nearest foreign neighbor.

FOREIGN TRADE. Although Australia possesses a diversity of natural resources and has a sophisticated industrial complex, its economy is by no means self-contained, and international trade has always been important to the well-being of the nation. The balance of export earnings with import payments has often been precarious, but in general the trade balance has been favorable through the years. Reciprocal trade agreements have been important stimulants to commerce, and as a result there is a complex pattern of preferential tariffs. The most preferential treatment is given to imports from New Zealand, the United Kingdom, and Canada, whereas various other countries of the British Commonwealth are granted preferences for certain items. Furthermore, intermediate tariffs are applied to certain goods from countries with which Australia has negotiated bilateral trade agreements, such as Japan, Germany, and Czechoslovakia.

Exports. Australia's principal exports have always been products from the pastoral, agricultural, and mining industries. Wool, wheat, and meat have been the traditional leaders, but in the past few years mineral ores have supplanted meat as the third leading export. Great Britain used to be the major customer for all of the principal exports but is no longer the leading consumer of any of them. Wool continues its dominance among Australian exports, accounting for a greater total value than the next four items (wheat, ores, meat, and sugar) combined. Japan has become the leading customer for Australian exports, normally buying from 20 per cent to 25 per cent of the total, with an emphasis on wool, iron ore, and coal. Although the British share is decreasing, it still buys about one-eighth of Australian exports, chiefly wool, gold, wheat, sugar, and butter. United

States purchases from Australia are approximately equal to those of Britain, with meat, sugar, wool, and lead ores as the principal items. Other customers—New Zealand, France, Italy, China—take much smaller proportions of total exports, but their share is significant in the aggregate. The export trend shows increasing sales to Japan and the United States, decreasing sales to Britain and other Commonwealth countries, and a conscious effort to exploit the relatively untapped markets of Asia, continental Europe, and South America.

Imports. The "colonial" character of Australia's foreign commerce is shown by comparing the composition of exports and imports. Whereas most of the former consists of raw materials and produce, the latter is composed largely of manufactured goods. The principal imports are machinery, motor vehicles and parts, chemicals, petroleum products, and textiles. During the latter half of the 1960's the United States surpassed the United Kingdom as principal supplier to Australia, their combined share of the import total exceeding 50 per cent and including a broad range of machinery, other metal products, chemicals, and consumer goods. Japan is now a strong third on the list of Australian suppliers, with emphasis on metal goods and textiles. Imports from Germany and Canada are also increasing. The significant import bill from Near Eastern countries and Indonesia is based almost entirely upon petroleum products.

Carriers. Most of the Australian overseas trade is handled by ships of other countries. Australian ships are rarely involved because their operating costs, especially wages, are too high to allow them to compete for the business. Much of the short-run commerce with so-called "adjacent islands," such as New Zealand, New Guinea, Norfolk Island, and Nauru, is carried in Australian bottoms, however.

Ports. A large number of ports have been developed in Australia, but, as with other economic activities, centrality is marked, and only a few ports handle the bulk of the traffic. Good natural harbors, such as those at Sydney and Hobart, are limited; thus a considerable amount of navigational assistance, dredging, and breakwater construction has been necessary. Many of the larger ports are located in or near the mouths of rivers, such as at Port Adelaide, Fremantle, Melbourne, and Newcastle; others are situated some distance upstream, as at Brisbane, Launceston, and Rockhampton; and there are a few exposed deep-sea ports, such as at Wollongong and Townsville, where extensive breakwaters must be built.

Sydney and Melbourne are by far the busiest ports on the continent. Between them they handle nearly half of all exports and about three-fourths of all imports. Port Adelaide, Brisbane, and Fremantle rank third, fourth, and fifth in imports, and fifth, third, and fourth in exports, respectively. No other Australian port handles as much as 5 per cent of total exports or imports, although the development of new ports in the northwest for shipping ores may change this pattern in the near future.

DIPLOMATIC AND MILITARY RELATIONS. Australia's foreign relations are governed largely by its geographical position, an isolated continent adjacent to Southeast Asia; its system of government, a federated democracy in a world split between two opposing power blocs; its background, one of strong historic-cultural ties with Britain; and its power base, a small population with an advanced economy. Its foreign policy has always been aimed at recognition of the need for a powerful ally, first Britain and now the United States. Since World War II Australia has made a conscious effort to strengthen relationships with the neighboring countries of southern and eastern Asia, but not at the expense of friendship with the powerful ally.

Australia has always been an active supporter of the United Nations in both principle and practice. She participates in most of the cultural, educational, and economic subsidiary organizations that have grown up around the U.N. As is common with many smaller powers, Australia is not as outwardly disappointed with U.N. failures as some of the larger nations are.

Furthermore, Australia has been a pillar of the British Commonwealth of Nations, that coterie of erstwhile British colonies whose leaders meet regularly to discuss common problems of international importance. It is not easy to assess the tangible benefits of belonging to the Commonwealth, as such membership does not involve either military alliance or trade treaty. Nevertheless, it provides a forum for airing viewpoints and espousing causes with other countries that have at least some common heritage, and as such it is probably a worthwhile link in international communication.

Since World War II Australia has been a participant in three formal alliances. (*1*) The Canberra Pact, a bilateral treaty with New Zealand, was promulgated before the war ended, in 1944, and marked the first occasion that these two countries had formalized mutual assistance. (*2*) The ANZUS pact was signed with the United States and New Zealand in 1951. It was originally designed as a mutual aid treaty to protect the Southwest Pacific area from resurgent Japanese militarism, but its more cogent function today is as a buffer against any threat from Red China. (*3*) Australia was a foundation signatory power of the Southeast Asia Treaty Organization (SEATO) in 1954, which was conceived as a deterrent to Communist expansion in southern and eastern Asia. The diverse nature and dispersed locations of the signatories (Australia, New Zealand, United States, United Kingdom, France, the Philippines, Thailand, Pakistan) have precluded much in the way of effective function.

Australia is also a foundation member of the Colombo Plan organization, which provides an umbrella to foster economic aid and development and thereby raise living standards and enhance political stability in the countries of southern and southeastern Asia. The plan provides that the fifteen "recipient" countries may work out cooperative enterprises of national development with each other and with the six "contributory" countries (Australia, Britain, Canada, New Zealand, United States, and Japan). Australia has been a major contributor to the plan, supplying an average of more than $7 million annually since it was organized in 1950, as well as training more than 6,000 Asian students in Australian universities and technical colleges.

Since World War II Australia has committed its military forces to three combat situations in Asia. Australian troop, air, and naval units fought with the other United Nations forces during the three years of the Korean conflict, suffering a total loss of about 300 men killed. Various Australian military units participated in the long-continuing pacification of insurgents in Malaysia, both on the Malay Peninsula and in North Borneo. The war in Viet Nam has engendered an Australian commitment of some 8,000 soldiers, about 10 per cent of the nation's rather small standing army.

Although Australia's formal alliances and tangible commitments have been farther afield, in many ways the most urgent aspect of foreign relations relates to Indonesia, the near neighbor to the north. With a population nearly nine times larger, and sharing Australia's only international land boundary (in New Guinea), Indonesia can be an important friend or a threatening enemy. During the presidency of the unpredictable and bellicose Sukarno, in the late 1950's and early 1960's, Indonesia's attitude was sporadically hostile and never friendly. After Sukarno was deposed, Indonesian-Australian relations were normalized, and there is now every evidence that both countries recognize the expediency of coexistence. Indeed, the foundations for a cordial relationship have been laid.

The Population Paradox in International Context

The changing world of the Australians is significantly affected by immigration patterns and policies. This large nation with a small population is pursuing an avowed goal of encouraging almost unrestricted immigration from Europe and North America, but severely restricting immigration from Asia and Africa. As was pointed out in Chapter 3, the Australian government has promulgated bilateral immigration schemes with a number of European countries, in a large number of instances providing "assisted passage" (inexpensive transportation) to the immigrant. There has thus been a steady flow of European migrants to Australia since World War II, the greatest number from Britain, but a considerable proportion from continental Europe. The intention of the Australian government is to maintain and accelerate this flow.

The non-British character of a large part of the present migrant stream has tended to leaven Australia's population mix considerably. There is a natural tendency to weaken ties with England and the Crown. Different languages are heard, an ethnic press has developed, new foods are appearing, and variety in customs and mores is growing. Many of the migrants assimilate only slowly into the Australian pattern of life; national clubs, cliques, and housing areas have become conspicuous.

Yet the population mix is not nearly as diverse as it might be, for there is a long history of immigration regulations that severely restrict the entrance of non-Caucasians into Australia. This so-called "white Australia" policy evolved during the middle of the nineteenth century, primarily as a nervous response to the deluge of Chinese who rushed to the gold diggings in Victoria and New South Wales and secondarily as a reaction against the cheap labor supplied by kanakas in Queensland. Implementation of the policy has not meant an absolute bar to Oriental or African immigration; indeed, in an average year between 500 and 1,000 Chinese become naturalized Australians, and about 5 per cent of all Australian immigrants come from Asia and Africa. Nevertheless, the effect of the policy is strongly inhibitory on non-European migration, and it is becoming a matter for increasing public discussion in Australia. No matter how fallacious the reasoning about Australia's empty acres in juxtaposition to Asia's teeming millions, it is probable that the immigration restrictions increase the difficulties in establishing smooth relations between Australia and her Asian neighbors. It is clear that any nation should have the right to determine its own immigration policy, and Australia would undoubtedly be foolish to hasten unduly the attraction of aliens who would be difficult to assimilate and thus provide the potential for racial problems. Nevertheless, as Australia strives to assume a comfortable stance as a "semi-Asian" country, increasing pressure, both internal and external, is going to develop for a broadening of the non-Caucasian immigration pattern.

An "Asian" Australia?

The "Asia-ness" of Australia is clearly a matter of debate. All of its near neighbors, with the exception of New Zealand, are Asiatic, and the weakening of ties with Britain has been contemporaneous with the strengthening of relationships with Asian countries. At the same time, it should be realized that Asia is an immense continent comprised of nearly four dozen countries. Australia's relationships have been mostly with the southeastern fringe, from Korea to Thailand, with nations that encompass barely 20 per cent of the continent's population. No matter what the rhetoric, Australia is a non-Asian nation situated next to Asia, "Western by heritage, Eastern by location." [1] Involvement with Asia is increasing, but there are still strong links with Europe, North America, and on a smaller scale, with the islands of the South Pacific.

The Pacific Island Neighborhood

Since very early in its settlement history, Australia has maintained a considerable interest in the islands to its north, northeast, and east. New Zealand, with its common heritage and history, has been a major focus of this interest. Papua and eastern New Guinea have commanded special attention because of Australia's administrative function and the small but vigorous group of Australian colonizers there. The smaller islands and island groups have for the most part been less significantly related to Australia, but in some instances the involvement has been notable.

New Guinea is not only a large land mass with a sizable population, it is also the island closest to Australia. Australia administers the eastern half of the island as the Territory of Papua and New Guinea, which also

[1] O. H. K. Spate, *Australia* (New York: Frederick A. Praeger, Inc., 1968), p. 308.

includes the nearby islands of New Britain, Bougainville, New Ireland, and Manus. The only larger "colonial" areas remaining in the world today are Danish Greenland and two Portuguese colonies in Africa. The economy of Papua and New Guinea is largely subsistence, and its commercial aspects are closely linked with Australia, from which considerable capital infusion is necessary to keep the economy viable. The official attitude of the Australian government is that in due course the people of the territory must decide their own political future, whether to become autonomous or to maintain some sort of affiliation with Australia. Preparation for that time of decision is difficult, given the rugged nature of the terrain, the primitive yet diverse characteristics of the population, and the elemental state of the economy. Progress toward self-determination is being made with deliberate speed, but external pressure (primarily from the United Nations) for haste has been mounting, and native aspirations are beginning to build up. Whatever the ultimate decision, however, Australia clearly will continue to have a close association with Papua and New Guinea.

Australia's relationships with the Pacific islands are, and have been, quite varied. She is a foundation member and major organizer of the South Pacific Commission, an organization established in 1947 by the six governments responsible for the administration of the island territories of the Pacific. The Commission, headquartered in New Caledonia, is primarily concerned with developmental works to bolster the economy, social welfare, and health of the islanders.

With respect to specific territories, Australia is closely associated with some and has little communication with others. There are intimate economic ties, for example, with Nauru (which markets much of its phosphate in Australia) and Fiji (whose monocultural sugar cane economy is a monopoly of a large Australian corporation). Furthermore, Australian currency is the medium of exchange in the Solomon Islands, Nauru, New Hebrides (in part), and the Gilbert and Ellice Islands Colony, and is at par with the new currency of Tonga. Of the relatively few Pacific islanders who are sent overseas for higher education or special training, a large proportion go to Australia, and Australian expatriates comprise much of the basic cadre of civil servants on many of the islands where English is an official language. Only in the French colonies, or in those islands with a special relationship with New Zealand (as Western Samoa and the Cook Islands) or the United States (as American Samoa and the islands of Micronesia), is Australian influence insignificant.

Although there is a lot of good-natured bantering to the contrary ("Australians are too rowdy and Americanized"; "New Zealanders are too reserved and formal"), the numerous similarities between the people of Australia and New Zealand and their shared proximate location in the southwestern Pacific have always engendered a close relationship between these two countries. Trade relationships between the two are unbalanced (a 4:1 ratio in Australia's favor) because their exports are largely competitive rather than complementary, and Australia's economy operates at a higher and broader based level. Australia is the second largest supplier of imports to New Zealand, whereas the latter ranks only eleventh on the list of Australian suppliers. The export pattern is more even. New Zealand is Australia's fourth largest customer, and Australia ranks fifth as a buyer of New Zealand goods. Apart from freight, there is a steady movement of both people and ideas across the Tasman Sea. Australia is by far the largest source of tourists to New Zealand (almost half of all short-term visitors to New Zealand are Australians), and New Zealanders comprise a significant share of all visitors to Australia. Furthermore, there is close diplomatic and military liaison between the two countries, and considerable mutual interest and concern among the respective citizenry.

CHAPTER 7

south pacific partner: new zealand

Southeast of Australia across the Tasman Sea is the island nation of New Zealand. Although the heritage and background of its population are essentially the same as the people of Australia, its environment is remarkably different and its economy is more circumscribed. New Zealand is a land of diverse and gentle beauty, with scenic splendors of many kinds. Its people lead a generally relaxed, middle-class life, with a relatively high standard of living and a democratic government that leans toward welfare state concepts. The natural resource supply is limited; therefore there is a narrow base for industrialization, and the economy is dangerously dependent upon export earnings from pastoral products.

Environmental Diversity

The broad uniformity that characterizes the Australian environment is lacking in New Zealand. Whereas large parts of Australia have an aspect of sameness, with almost monotonous expanses of flat land and sweeping vistas, the New Zealand horizon is typically interrupted by sloping land and dense vegetation. Thus macro-generalizations about the physical geography of New Zealand are not very meaningful, and a real understanding of the environment requires analysis of the micro-aspects of exposure and altitude.

TERRAIN: DOMINANCE OF SLOPE. New Zealand occupies an unstable section of the earth's crust, a position along the "Pacific Rim of Fire" where mountain building and other forms of crustal disturbance have been relatively active during recent geologic eras. Two conspicuous undersea mountain arcs come together in the North Island, one trending southeasterly from New Guinea and New Caledonia via the Northland peninsula and the other southwesterly from Tonga and the Kermadec Islands into East Cape (Figure 7-1). The mountain trends continue southwesterly the length of the country, but the pattern of ranges is irregular and discontinuous for the most part and is repeatedly interrupted by many narrow valleys and a few broad plains.

The North Island basically consists of hilly country underlain by relatively weak rock, although there is a hardrock mountain core extending northeast-southwest along the eastern side of the island. The surface expression of the core is mostly hill land consisting of several disconnected ranges, separated by small plains and basins. In the center of the island there is a conspicuous volcanic region containing dissected plateaus, notable volcanic peaks, a complex of hydrothermal features, and New Zealand's largest lake. Lake Taupo is nearly twice as large as any other lake in the country, and its river system (the Upper Waikato River drains into the south end of the lake and the Waikato River drains out to the north) is easily the longest in New Zealand, as well as being the principal source of hydroelectricity for the North Island. On the south side of the lake are three prominent volcanic peaks, all active, whose summits range from 6,500 to 9,200 feet above sea level. Vulcanism on the north side of the lake is manifested by a multitude of geysers, hot springs, fumaroles, and geothermal steam vents. The northern portion of the North Island is characterized by more gentle terrain, with rolling country alternating with flattish plains in the Waikato District and the Northland peninsula. The dominant topographic feature of the western part of the island is the symmetrical cone of Mt. Egmont, which rises abruptly to 8,300 feet above the fringing Taranaki lowland.

The South Island is not only larger, but also more mountainous and rugged than the North Island. However, its volcanic manifestations are fewer. The massive mountain chain known as the Southern Alps makes up the backbone of the island and occupies about half of its surface area. The bedrock composition of the chain consists of relatively hard rocks, especially gneiss and greywacke (a sort of sandstone). The highest and most spectacular portion of the Alps is in the center of the chain, particularly around Mt. Cook (12,350 feet) and Mt. Aspiring (9,950 feet), where extensive snowfields occur and lengthy glaciers reach down west side valleys almost to tidewater. In the north of the island the main chain of the Alps divides into a confused sequence of discrete ranges, most of which trend northeast-southwest and are separated by longitudinal valleys. These ranges are lower, unglaciated, and less rugged. The southern portion of the Alps also breaks up into a mixed pattern of ranges and valleys; elevations are lower there, but the mountains have been carved into a remarkable series of steep-sided valleys and fiords by past glacial action. The western slope of the entire chain of the Southern Alps is marked by an abrupt, often precipitous, descent to the coast, with almost no coastal plain. On the eastern side, in contrast, there are extensive foothills, longitudinal glaciated valleys (many of them occupied by deep, fresh water lakes), vast areas covered with "shingle" (glacio-fluvial outwash of sand and gravel), and a number of intricately braided rivers. In the east central

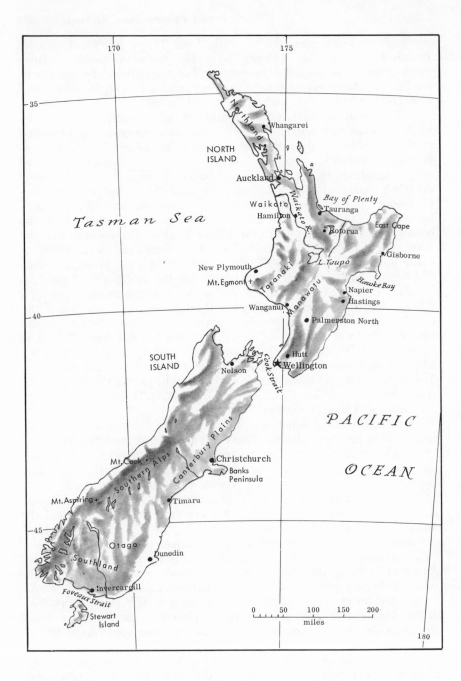

Figure 7-1 New Zealand

portion of the South Island is the Canterbury Plains, the only extensive lowland area in New Zealand. It is a piedmont alluvial plain veneered deeply with shingle and crossed by many southeast-flowing rivers. Banks Peninsula is a partially worn down volcanic mass that extends as the only major protrusion into the Pacific Ocean. The southeastern portion of the South Island is an irregularly dissected section comprising the Otago and Southland districts. Otago is mostly hill country, and Southland contains a number of small plains and basins separated by hills.

CLIMATE: A WELL-WATERED LAND.   New Zealand's climate is the type classified as Marine West Coast, that is, a mid-latitude climate dominated by moist air from the ocean. Only on the east (leeward) side of major mountains is there sufficient protection from oceanic air to produce a relatively dry environment. The principal climatic determinants are latitude, altitude, exposure, prevailing winds, and the maritime surroundings. The mid-latitude location of New Zealand (34° to 47° south) dictates that westerly winds generally sweep the islands, bringing a year-round pattern of irregular cyclonic storms and meridional fronts.

Precipitation is moderate to abundant over most of New Zealand; average annual figures of 30 to 60 inches typify most of the settled parts of the country. Mountainous areas receive more moisture, of course; much of the high country gets more than 100 inches annually, and a fairly extensive section of the west side of the Southern Alps records in excess of 200 inches. The "rain shadow" position of the Canterbury and Otago districts, on the leeward side of the Alps, inhibits precipitation so that many places receive less than 25 inches annually and a few localities get less than 15 inches. The seasonal regime of precipitation is fairly regular throughout the year, with a tendency toward a winter maximum on the North Island and a slight summer maximum on the South Island. Most of the precipitation is frontal in origin, with obvious orographic effects in mountainous and hilly areas. There is some notable convectional rain in summer, particularly in inland sections of the South Island. Snowfall is uncommon in the North Island and in the lowlands of the South Island, but is quite heavy in the mountains.

Temperatures are generally moderate except in the mountains. In most settled parts of the country one may expect summer temperatures to range between 50° and 80°, with winter temperatures varying between 30° and 70°. No significant town has ever experienced a temperature above 100° or below 10°, although much lower minima can be expected in the mountains. The normally high level of relative humidity tends to emphasize the cooler temperatures rather than the warmer ones.

There is a fairly high degree of windiness in most parts of New Zealand. This condition is particularly noticeable in the mountains and in some coastal areas, as along the shores of Cook Strait.

NATURAL VEGETATION: VARIETY IN ABUNDANCE.   The natural vegetation patterns of New Zealand are more complex than those of Australia, with much greater local variations in distribution. Furthermore, the plant communities of New Zealand have been relatively unstable, that is, in a state of change, during recent geologic eras because of vagaries of nature (volcanic activity and glaciation) and within historic time because of human activities (fires, heavy grazing, land clearance).

Mixed broadleaf-podocarp forests originally covered most of the North Island and much of the western side of the Alps. These were generally classed as modified rain forests, occurring in dense stands and containing an abundance of ferns and treeferns. Southern beech forests (*Nothofagus*) were notable in much of the South Island and were found in scattered parts of the North Island as well.

Throughout much of New Zealand there were many areas dominated by scrub and fern scrub. Such growth characteristically occurred where the soils were less fertile or where recent vulcanism or fire had interfered with forest development. Overall, scrub communities were much more widespread on the North Island than on the South. The boundaries between forest and scrub land were both irregular and subject to rapid fluctuation; with a respite from burning the forest advanced, and with increased burning the scrub advanced.

Some large areas were grass covered. Tussock grassland was common east of the Alps in the South Island and in some of the volcanic heartland of the North Island. Alpine grasslands, or tundra, were characteristic above the treeline on higher mountains.

Much of the native vegetation has been removed or replaced in recent years; partially by clearing for agriculture, but much more significantly by firing and overgrazing. Most of the pasture land of New Zealand today has been seeded to exotic grasses introduced from various parts of the world.

FAUNA: SCARCE OR EXOTIC.   Whereas the native animal life of Australia can be characterized as unique and bizarre, that of New Zealand is best described as "absent." Indigenous terrestrial animals were almost entirely missing; there were no land mammals at all, no reptiles except for a few species of lizard, no amphibians except for a few frogs. Avian fauna, on the other hand, was conspicuous and dominant. Sea birds were the most common, but there were many other varieties. A distinctive feature of the bird life was the relatively high proportion of flightless birds. The most notable of these was the moa, which finally died out just before the European discovery of New Zealand. The largest of the two dozen species of moa grew to a height of twelve feet.

The absence of native animal life encouraged the European settlers to import exotic forms from many parts of the world. Indeed, New Zealand has become the world's most notable example of a land wherein exotic animals dominate the fauna. Some thirty species of birds, fifteen species of mammals, and a number of fish from other continents have become established members of the New Zealand biota. Several varieties of deer have become so common that they have assumed the role of pests and are systematically destroyed by government employed deer cullers. There are also thriving populations of American elk, European chamois, and Asiatic tahr (a type of mountain goat). A variety of furbearers has also become established in New Zealand. Most notable are European rabbits (which had assumed plague proportions in some areas before myxomatosis was introduced), Australian possums (a major destroyer of trees in the North Island) and wallabies, and a variety of rats and mice. The folly of introducing exotic fauna without adequate planning is demonstrated clearly in New Zealand.

The Human Occupancy

The prehistory of New Zealand is still very imperfectly understood. From the limited archaeological evidence that is available, we can infer that the magnificent landscape of these islands was untrammeled by human footsteps until much later than almost any other portion of the earth's land surface. It is believed that New Zealand remained unoccupied by man until well after the beginning of the Christian era.

PRE-EUROPEAN SETTLERS.   The first humans to settle in New Zealand apparently were wandering Polynesians who arrived between 1,000 and 2,000 years ago. Where they came from and how they reached New Zealand is unclear. Their scanty archeological remains indicate a distribution pattern that tended to concentrate in east coastal settlements on the South Island, although certainly the North Island was populated as well. They were peaceful, rather primitive people, whose economy was based essentially on bird hunting and fishing. Apparently their principal quarry was the giant moa, and the people have therefore often been referred to simply as "Moa-hunters," although some scholars prefer the term "Archaic Maoris."

The relationship between the Archaic Maoris of earlier times and the Classic Maoris who occupied New Zealand at the time of European contact is as yet unknown. It is probable that the Moa-hunter culture developed into the Classic Maori culture through a normal process of cultural evolution, although from time to time the population mix was enriched by the abrupt addition of newcomers, who were usually Polynesian immigrants arriving from islands far to the north or northeast. There is considerable evidence that a final wave of immigration arrived during a relatively short time span in the fourteenth century, giving notable external stimulus to the development of the Classic Maori culture.

In any event, the Classic Maoris differed considerably from the Moa-hunters. Their economy was more advanced (including systematic agriculture), and they were more warlike. Although they spread widely over New Zealand, the warmer climate of the northern areas suited them best, and the principal population concentrations were in the northern part of the North Island. By the time of European contact, in the late eighteenth century, their occupancy pattern had been stabilized, and their numbers were estimated to be between 150,000 and 250,000.

At that time more than 80 per cent of the Maoris lived in the northern half of the North Island. Their economy was significantly agricultural, with the kumara (*Ipomoea batatas*), a sort of sweet potato, as their principal crop. Also, they spent much time in gathering fernroot, in fishing, and in hunting for birds. For the most part they lived in scattered hamlets, and occasionally in fortified refuges, called "pa." They were divided into a large number of politically autonomous tribes, each with a more or less recognized territory. The tribes were generally grouped into a number of loosely knit intertribal associations, and intergroup warfare was frequent, if not incessant.

Most of the remainder of the Maori population, perhaps 15 per cent of the total, settled in the southern half of the North Island and along the north coast of the South Island. They were more dependent upon hunting, fishing, and gathering than they were upon agriculture; their settlements were generally smaller and less permanent; and they were less warlike.

Most of the South Island was very sparsely settled, although some Maori settlements were found as far south as Stewart Island. The South Island Maoris had a primitive subsistence economy.

ARRIVAL OF THE EUROPEANS.   The first Europeans came in Tasman's two Dutch ships in 1642. Tasman coasted most of New Zealand's western margin, but he did not land. His one attempt resulted in the spearing of four of his sailors. After Tasman there was a 127-year hiatus before other Europeans visited New Zealand. Captain James Cook arrived in 1769, spent six months exploring the coastline, completely circumnavigated both islands, and developed relatively peaceful relations with several tribes of the truculent Maoris. Cook also called at New Zealand during his second and third voyages to the Pacific in the 1770's, and other explorers, British, French, and Spanish, came as well.

The first European settlement was a sealing station established on the west coast of the South Island in 1792, and several other sealing and whaling stations were opened during the subsequent four decades. These temporary settlements became more permanent and more numerous, although New Zealand still was not officially claimed by any colonial power. Deserters from ships and escaped convicts from Australia made up a significant proportion of the small European population; lawlessness was rampant, and there was sporadic fighting with the Maoris.

Missionaries and others were eager to establish viable settlements, but all of the early attempts failed. Finally, in 1840, the first true colonization settlement was established at Wellington by the New Zealand Company, under the stimulus of Edward Gibbon Wakefield, the man who had organized the South Australian colony a few years earlier. In that same year British sovereignty was proclaimed over New Zealand. By 1850 there were eight separate settlements in New Zealand, five on the North Island and three on the South. Also by that time most of the Maori tribes had managed to obtain guns, so that their intertribal wars became more deadly. It is estimated that they managed to reduce their population, largely through internecine warfare, by 40 or 50 per cent during the second quarter of the nineteenth century.

THE SPREAD OF SETTLEMENT.   The second half of the nineteenth century in New Zealand, as in Australia, was a time of rapid population increase and settlement expansion. Furthermore, during this period the tide of settlement shifted from the North Island to the South Island and back again.

In the early 1850's the North Island population, both European and Maori, was considerably greater than that of the South Island. The Europeans, with only a handful of exceptions, were concentrated on the coasts —Russell, Auckland, New Plymouth, Wanganui, and Wellington on the North Island; Nelson, Christchurch, and Dunedin on the South Island. The interior was largely Maori country; both danger from the natives and lack of economic stimulus served to discourage European penetration inland. The introduction of sheep was the first factor influencing a change in the pattern. The prospect of wool production lured some hardy settlers away from the coast, but a relatively few men claimed most of the land.

Gold was discovered in inland Otago in 1861, signaling a major reorientation in both the economy and demography of New Zealand. There was a great migration to the South Island from the North Island, from Australia, and from overseas. Within less than a decade Otago had one-fourth of New Zealand's population, and its principal town, Dunedin, numbered some 60,000 inhabitants, making it by far the largest settlement in the colony. Later, alluvial gold was found on the beaches of Westland, and the South Island gold boom continued to be significant until about 1875.

Meanwhile, on the North Island there were increasing attempts at inland settlement by Europeans. The alienation of Maori land brought about a sharp increase in hostilities between Europeans and natives, and the entire decade of the 1860's was marked by the "Maori wars," which resulted in inevitable defeat of the Maoris (except for some who sided with the government) and a rapid diffusion of European land ownership in the interior of the island.

European population growth and settlement expansion were more rapid in the South Island, however, as there was only a small native population to negotiate with. The Canterbury Plains became an important agricultural area in the 1870's and 1880's, emphasizing wheat; this was the most significant period of wheat cultivation in New Zealand history.

Perhaps the most important event in the economic history of New Zealand was the inauguration of refrigerated shipping in 1882. Until that time the principal exports had been such nonperishable items as wool, tallow, wheat, and gold. With refrigeration, however, meat and dairy products could be added to the list. Whereas most New Zealand sheep had been Merinos, raised strictly for their wool, mutton and lamb could now be produced. Accordingly, dual-purpose breeds became more important, with the varieties known as Romney Marsh (imported from Britain) and Corriedale (developed in New Zealand) soon dominating.

Much of the interior of both islands, apart from that continually diminishing area still under Maori control in the North Island, was held in a relatively few large estates. This pattern of land tenure came under increasingly severe pressure. Squatters settled in many places with little consideration of the legality of their action. However, some of the large estates were broken up voluntarily, and legislation in the 1890's provided for compulsory subdivision of most of the remainder. The relatively dense growth of forest and bush over much of the North Island was an impediment, but vast acreages were cleared in a relatively short time. Land clearance was less significant on the South Island.

In terms of population concentration, the pendulum had swung north again, perhaps never to change. The rate of population growth on the North Island was faster than that on the South during the last two decades of the nineteenth century, and by the dawn of the twentieth century the North Island contained more than half of New Zealand's total population. The spread and intensification of settlement continued to be faster on the North Island, depending primarily upon fat-lamb raising and dairy production of butter and cheese for export. By early in this century most of New Zealand's usable land was occupied.

Contemporary New Zealand

Twentieth century New Zealand has evolved in an orderly and systematic fashion into a modern and progressive nation. Despite a serious lack of natural resources, a general balance has been obtained in the domestic economy. The export structure, on the other hand, is highly unbalanced, and heavy continuing dependence upon a few primary products is a source of perennial worry. New Zealanders as a whole enjoy a pleasant life that is somewhat more sedate than that of Australians. The pace of business is slower; opportunities to accumulate considerable wealth are quite limited, but true poverty is almost unknown.

THE POPULACE.   As the decade of the 1970's begins, the population of New Zealand is about 3,000,000. It is growing at a rate of 2 to 2½ per cent per year, an annual gain of about 60,000 people. Natural increase accounts for most of the population increment, although there is a continuing net immigration that usually averages from 10,000 to 15,000 per year.

Following a trend that began almost a century ago, the population continues to concentrate on the North Island. Today about 70 per cent of all New Zealanders live there, in comparison to less than 50 per cent at the turn of the century. Most of the population resides in cities and towns, although this tendency is not as pronounced as it is in Australia. Approximately 75 per cent of the population is classed as urban (residing in cities or towns with a population exceeding 1,000); the urban proportion is higher on the North Island than it is on the South.

Four principal urban areas are significantly larger than any others—Auckland, Wellington-Hutt, Christchurch, and Dunedin (see Figure 7-1). Together these four contain about 45 per cent of the total population, a measure of centralization that is almost as great as in the four largest Australian cities. Metropolitan *Auckland* has a population of some 600,000. It is the principal commercial and industrial center of the nation, has the busiest port, and is the only New Zealand city with the cosmopolitan characteristics of similar sized cities in other countries. *Wellington* is the national capital and, with its suburbs in the Hutt Valley, sprawls around three sides of the spacious bay called Wellington Harbour. The combined population of Wellington-Hutt is about 300,000. Almost as large is *Christchurch*, the principal city of the South Island and hub of the fertile Canterbury Plains. *Dunedin*, the long-established commercial center of the Otago District, contains about 125,000 people.

Thirteen other cities are officially classed as "urban areas" in New Zealand, but none of them is even half as large as Dunedin. They range in size from Hamilton, the fast-growing regional center of the Waikato District (with a population of about 70,000), to Nelson, an old port town in a fertile farming area on the north coast of the South Island (population about 30,000). The rural population is broadly scattered over the productive parts of the country, and thus is found primarily in lowland areas. The principal rural population concentrations are in the rolling country of the Waikato District south of Auckland, in the Taranaki lowland around Mt. Egmont, in the broad Manawatu lowland around Palmerston North, in the northern and central portions of the Canterbury Plains, and in the rolling coastal hinterlands of Dunedin and Invercargill.

The Maoris comprise a small but significant minority within the population, making up the only conspicuous non-European element. At the beginning of this century there were only about 40,000 Maoris; today the total is approximately 200,000,[1] divided about equally between full-bloods and half-castes. These figures indicate a rapid rate of increase in recent decades. The Maoris characteristically have a high birth rate, giving them a net rate of increase that is twice as great as that of the non-Maori population. About 95 per cent of the people with Maori blood live on the North Island, mostly in the northern part. More than two-thirds of them live in rural areas, but in recent years there has been a decided drift to the cities. The Maoris ostensibly have equal rights with any other New Zealanders, and, despite their generally low economic position, they have made reasonable progress toward amalgamation with the general population.

The New Zealand government actively encourages immigration from European countries and has worked out assisted passage schemes with several nations. The population gain from immigration fluctuates widely from year to year, but normally shows a net growth of several thousand. Migrants from the United Kingdom dominate the flow, usually amounting to more than one-half of the total. Other major contributors to net immigration are Australia (10 per cent of the total) and the Netherlands (5 per cent).

THE ECONOMY. New Zealand's economy is dominated by its rural industries, especially animal husbandry. Although the majority of the labor force is employed in secondary and tertiary activities, these are supported by a narrow resource base, and sheep raising, dairying, and beef production are the basic supports of the economy. The domestic

[1] All persons with half or more of Maori blood are defined as Maoris for statistical purposes.

market is not large enough to absorb all of the butter, wool, mutton, lamb, beef, veal, and cheese produced; thus, overseas sales take about two-thirds of the output.

Gross farm income is divided approximately as follows: one-half from pastoral products, one-third from dairy products, and one-sixth from crops. Furthermore, more than 90 per cent of the nation's exports consist of animal products. In a real sense, then, New Zealand's economy is dependent upon the nutritious pasture grasses that have been introduced to replace the indigenous vegetation. The country's economic history has been dominated by the prosaic but continuing struggle to clear the bush and plant new grasses.

Pastoralism. The leading rural industry is sheep raising. New Zealand's 60,000,000 sheep are widely spread, but the greatest concentrations and the more intensive activities are on the North Island, where some 60 per cent of the total is found. Most North Island sheep farms are relatively small (1,000 to 3,000 acres), graze a few hundred or a few thousand head of sheep on improved pastures, and produce both wool and meat as major products. In many cases, particularly in the northern part of the island, sheep raising and dairying are carried out on the same farm. On the South Island nearly half of the sheep are maintained on extensive, high-country "runs," where woolly Merinos are dominant. On the Canterbury Plains and in some of the smaller lowlands of the South Island, large numbers of sheep are kept in mixed farming enterprises, which are similar in many ways to operations in the Australian wheat-sheep belt.

Dairying. The 7,000,000 cattle in New Zealand are divided approximately equally between dairy and beef types. Dairying, however, is second only to sheep raising among the nation's leading agricultural activities. The principal dairy areas are in the northern third of the North Island, from the Bay of Plenty coastland and the Waikato District northward. Other major dairying concentrations are in the Taranaki lowland and in the Manawatu area around Palmerston North. Most of the dairying country was originally forested; the productive pastures of the present are almost completely the result of clearing the land and planting exotic grasses.

Other agriculture. Other agricultural activities of significance are the growing of crops and the raising of beef cattle and pigs. Most crops are grown in mixed crop-and-livestock operations which have meat as a significant farm product. The South Island contains more than four-fifths of the total crop acreage, mostly in the Canterbury Plains and the coastal lowlands of Otago. The major cash crops are wheat, oats, barley, and potatoes, and much acreage is devoted to the growing of such items as turnips, swedes, and peas for stock feed; however, most of the farmland is sown to grasses and clovers for grazing. There is also a certain amount of market gardening and orcharding, particularly around Auckland and Hawke Bay on the North Island and around Nelson on the South Island. Almost all of these intensively grown crops are destined for domestic consumption; apples constitute the only New Zealand crop that is exported significantly.

Power development. Although New Zealand is essentially without petroleum and natural gas, and its coal resources are sparse and poor, electric power generation is one of the few strengths in its resource inventory. The high elevations, steep slopes, and abundant rainfall produce many natural lakes and swift streams, which offer a high potential for hydroelectric power. The development and utilization of this potential has been imaginatively and extensively accomplished, so that a first-class, interconnected power grid blankets both islands, and the per capita consumption of electric energy in New Zealand is one of the highest in the world. There are some large coal deposits, notably the bituminous fields on the west coast of the South Island and subbituminous reserves in the Waikato District, but most of the supplies occur in a fragmented pattern, and both mining and transportation costs are high. Nevertheless, some coal is used for thermal-electric generation, and geothermal steam power has been harnessed for electricity production in the Wairakei area just north of Lake Taupo.

Extractive industries.   The paucity of resources makes extractive industries insignificant in the economy. Apart from coal, New Zealand's mineral resources are very limited, with gold being the only other mineral of importance. Timber resources are also sparse, partly owing to excessive cutting in the past. However, a number of exotic pine (mostly *Pinus radiata* from California) plantations have been developed, yielding more than half of the nation's total cut of sawn timber, and providing the basis for a small but rapidly expanding pulp and paper industry. Commercial fishing has always been minor, but recent expansion, particularly in crayfish and oysters, has been impressive.

Urban activities.   Secondary and tertiary activities are very important, but there is little distinctive about their development. New Zealand possesses the range of commercial and service industries that should be expected of a small country with a high standard of living. The scope of these activities is strictly limited to satisfying the domestic demand.

Manufacturing industries are similarly limited. Although more than 200,000 people, amounting to more than one-fourth of the labor force, are employed in manufacturing, this segment of the economy has depended very heavily upon government encouragement and protection for its growth. Protective tariffs, customs duties, and import restrictions have made it possible for a wide range of manufacturing industries to develop, many of which would not be viable in an unprotected environment. Analysis of the industrial structure further emphasizes the restricted role of secondary industry. The principal type of manufacturing, by far, is the processing of agricultural produce, which employs almost 25 per cent of the entire manufacturing work force. The second ranking industry is the manufacture of wood products, which employs less than 10 per cent of all manufacturing workers. Other leading types of manufacturing are paper products, printing and publishing, and apparel making. The manufacturing segment of the economy is becoming increasingly important, but its position continues to be protected by government paternalism.

Foreign trade.   New Zealand's external trade patterns are generally simple and unchanging. Throughout its short history the country has been dependent upon foreign trade for its development, and for most of this time the trading patterns have been distinctly "colonial," involving the export of primary foodstuffs and raw materials and the import of manufactured goods. For more than a century Great Britain has been both the principal customer and the leading supplier. The per capita value of New Zealand's foreign trade is one of the highest in the world, a fact that emphasizes the relative importance of trade to the economy.

All of New Zealand's principal exports are pastoral products. Wool and meat are easily the two leading exports; in most years each comprises nearly 30 per cent of total exports. Butter, cheese, and other dairy products combined amount to more than 25 per cent of all exports, but no other item makes up as much as 3 per cent of the total. Great Britain purchases nearly half of New Zealand's exports, taking almost all of the butter, cheese, and lamb. The United States, Japan, France, Australia, and West Germany are other leading customers, in that order. Britain supplies about one-third of New Zealand's imports; other significant suppliers are Australia, the United States, and Japan.

New Zealand's trade pattern has begun to change in the last few years. There is little difference in the composition of the trade, except for increasing export of pulp and paper products. The direction of trade is shifting, however; Britain's share of both exports and imports is slowly declining, whereas the trade volume with Japan, the United States, and several countries of Western Europe is increasing.

THE OUTLOOK.   The overriding consideration in an assessment of New Zealand's future is the perilous position of the economy. Heavy dependence upon export of primary products to balance the steady flow of needed imports has always been a delicate matter and has required astute governmental management. Great Britain's attempt to join the European Economic Community has presented New Zealand with the spectre of losing its favored position in the British market, which would be a staggering blow to New Zealand's balance of trade. If Britain were to become a member of the Common Market, she would immediately begin to purchase less New Zealand meat and dairy products, and this decline would present domestic producers with severe economic hardship. New Zealand's economic planners hope that Britain's application will be delayed long enough so that substitute markets can be developed; however, substitutes of sufficient magnitude may be hard to find.

New Zealand shares Australia's external political problems, associated with a position near Southeast Asia and an immigration policy that excludes most non-Caucasians. She is also a participant in the same diplomatic and military ventures, such as Colombo Plan, SEATO, and the Vietnam War, and strives to maintain close ties with Britain while strengthening relations with the United States.

New Zealand is a pleasant, attractive, quiet, happy land. If it can somehow find alternate markets for its primary produce, it is likely to remain that way, provided the limited warfare in Southeast Asia does not spread.

a selected bibliography
of basic works

Periodicals

Australian Geographer. Geographical Society of New South Wales, Sydney.
Australian Geographical Studies. Institute of Australian Geographers, Hobart.
New Zealand Geographer. New Zealand Geographical Society, Christchurch.
Pacific Islands Monthly. Pacific Publications Pty. Ltd., Sydney.
Pacific Viewpoint. University of Wellington, Wellington.
South Pacific Bulletin. South Pacific Commission, Sydney.

Atlases

Atlas of Australian Resources. Canberra: Dept. of National Development, various dates.
Atlas of New Zealand Geography, G. J. R. LINGE and R. M. FRAZER. Wellington: A. H. & A. W. Reed, 1965.
Descriptive Atlas of New Zealand, A. H. MCLINTOCK (ed.). Wellington: Government Printer, 1960.
Descriptive Atlas of the Pacific Islands. T. F. KENNEDY. Wellington: A. H. & A. W. Reed, 1966.

Yearbooks and Handbooks

Handbook of Fiji, JUDY TUDOR (ed.). Sydney: Pacific Publications Pty. Ltd., irregular.
Handbook of Papua and New Guinea, JUDY TUDOR (ed.). Sydney: Pacific Publications Pty. Ltd., irregular.
New Zealand Official Yearbook. Wellington, Government Printer, annual.
Pacific Islands Year Book and Who's Who, JUDY TUDOR (ed.). Sydney: Pacific Publications Pty. Ltd., issued about every 3 years.
Year Book of the Commonwealth of Australia. Canberra: Commonwealth Bureau of Census and Statistics, annual.

Books

C.S.I.R.O., *The Australian Environment*, London: Cambridge University Press, 1960.

CUMBERLAND, K. B., *Southwest Pacific*, Christchurch: Whitcombe & Tombs, 1960.

FOX, J. W., and K. B. CUMBERLAND, *New Zealand: A Regional View*, Christchurch: Whitcombe & Tombs, 1958.

GRATTAN, C. H., *The Southwest Pacific since 1900*, Ann Arbor, Mich.: University of Michigan Press, 1963.

――――, *The Southwest Pacific to 1900*, Ann Arbor, Mich.: University of Michigan Press, 1963.

HUXLEY, ELSPETH, *Their Shining Eldorado: A Journey through Australia*, London: Chatto & Windus Ltd., 1967.

LASERON, C. F., *The Face of Australia*, Sydney: Angus & Robertson, 1957.

NAVAL INTELLIGENCE DIVISION (U. K.), *Pacific Islands* (4 volumes), London: 1945.

OLIVER, DOUGLAS L., *The Pacific Islands*, Garden City, N. Y.: Doubleday & Company, Inc., 1961.

REES, HENRY, *Australasia*, London: MacDonald & Evans, 1964.

ROBINSON, K. W., *Australia, New Zealand and the Southwest Pacific*, London: University of London Press, 1962.

ROSE, A. J., *Dilemmas Down Under*, Princeton, N. J.: D. van Nostrand Co., 1966.

SPATE, O. H. K., *Australia*, New York: Frederick A. Praeger, Inc., 1969.

TAYLOR, GRIFFITH, *Australia*, London: Methuen & Co., 1958.

TWEEDIE, ALAN, and K. W. ROBINSON, *The Regions of Australia*, Croydon, Victoria: Longmans, Green & Co. Ltd., 1963.

WADHAM, WILSON, and WOOD, *Land Utilization in Australia*, Melbourne: Melbourne University Press, 1957.

WATTERS, R. F. (ed.), *Land and Society in New Zealand*, Wellington: A. H. & A. W. Reed, 1965.

DATE DUE